SAILING

Gretel, an Australian challenger for the America's Cup in final trials in Sydney in 1962.

Cover (hardback edition): Maverick at Cowes.

Front endpaper (cover, paperback edition): *The Italian yacht* Ydra, *USA's* America Jane II, *Ireland's* Golden Apple *and* Ciel III *sport fantastic spinnakers during the One Ton Cup.*

Back endpaper (hardback edition): *A gaff ketch stems the tide during an autumn sunset in the Solent.*

INTERNATIONAL LIBRARY

ROBIN KNOX-JOHNSTON

SAILING

COLLINS · PUBLISHERS   FRANKLIN WATTS, INC.

London · Glasgow   New York

From top to bottom:
Henrietta, Vesta *and*
Fleetwing *sail in an*
early race.
Pinta *of Germany.*
Edward VII's
Britannia.
An Admiral's Cup
Race in 1973.

© *1977 International Library*
© *1977 William Collins Sons and Company Limited*

First Edition 1977

ISBN 0 00 100178 7 (*Collins cased edition*)
ISBN 0 00 103332 8 (*Collins paperback edition*)
SBN 531 02125 4 (*Watts*)

CONTENTS

Chapter 1
INTRODUCTION . . . . *page* 7

Chapter 2
DINGHIES AND HOW TO
SAIL THEM 19

Chapter 3
MULTIHULLS AND
EXPERIMENTAL CRAFT . . 35

Chapter 4
CRUISING 47

Chapter 5
OCEAN RACING 61

Chapter 6
THE AMERICA'S CUP . . . 77

Chapter 7
THE OLYMPIC CLASSES . . 97

Chapter 8
EPIC VOYAGES 111

FURTHER READING . . . 126

INDEX 127

INTRODUCTION

Boats built for pleasure or recreation have existed from ancient times. One of the earliest on record was Cleopatra's barge: the Venetian States had State yachts, and more recently Queen Elizabeth I of England had the oddly named *Rat of Wight* built at Cowes in 1588. These craft were reserved for the use of kings and emperors, however, and the building of small sailcraft solely for pleasure, in the modern sense, first started in Holland in the early part of the 17th century. There, waterways were as common as roads and the more wealthy burghers began to build private boats as a means of transportation, much as in other countries they had the coach and horse.

These boats were small and light, built for a speed and the manœuvrability necessary for sailing in constricted waterways. They came to be called "hunters", or in Dutch "*jachts*", the origin of the word "yacht" now used throughout the world to describe pleasure craft. By the middle of the 17th century the ports of Holland were thronged with gaily painted yachts. Almost all of them were built to resemble miniature men-of-war, reflecting the national pride in the Dutch fleet, then one of the mightiest in Europe.

Yachting remained a solely Dutch sport until the restoration of the British monarchy in 1660 when Charles II, who had lived in Holland during his exile and grown to enjoy the sport, returned to the throne. As a coronation present the Dutch States presented him with a 15 metre (50 foot) yacht called *Mary*, and it is recorded that she cost "1,300 pounds sterling" to build!

Between 1661 and 1663 five more royal yachts were built either for the King or his brother James, Duke of York, who had also caught sea fever. The earliest record of racing in England was noted by diarist John Evelyn who wrote:

Opposite:
Edward VII's Britannia, *one of the fastest yachts of her time. His nephew, the German Kaiser Wilhelm II, was so impressed by his uncle's yacht he had one designed especially to race against her.*

Charles II, King of Britain from 1660 to 1685.

"October 1st 1661 . . . I had sailed this morning with his Majesty in one of the yachts or pleasure boats, being very excellent sailing vessels. It was on a wager between his other new pleasure boat, built frigate-like and one of the Duke of York's; the wager one hundred pounds sterling; the race from Greenwich to Gravesend and back. The king lost in going, the wind being contrary, but saved stakes in returning."

Charles's addiction to the sport threatened the substance of the English fleet which was paid for out of the same purse.

But in its early days yachting did not exist for racing. The boats were diminutive men-of-war and spent their time forming up to perform naval manœuvres, going so far as to fire their miniature cannon at each other. Charles and his brother formed their own fleets, shortly to be followed by many others. From these fleets, with their admirals, commodores, rear commodores and so on, the modern yacht club developed. The first such club, the Cork Water Club, now the Royal Cork Yacht Club, was founded in Ireland in 1720.

Inevitably, as the number of yachts grew owners became interested in speed and began asking designers to improve on the rather sluggish lines which had been developed as the result of copying warships built more for carrying guns and withstanding shot than for speed. Fast small boats abounded in commercial use around the English coastline. Fishermen used small ruggedly built cutters, and faster versions of these were used by both smugglers and Revenue agents. Yachtsmen began to build copies of these cutters, but they still carried guns and went in for naval-style manœuvres.

Although racing does not appear to have been the original occupation of the yachtsmen, and short cruises of no longer than a day satisfied most, in 1749 the Duke of Cumberland's fleet raced from Greenwich on the Thames to the Nore in Kent and back, for a plate presented by the Prince of Wales. This is the earliest recorded non-royal yacht race, and within a few years racing to definite rules within the Cumberland fleet had become commonplace. This fleet later became today's Royal Thames Yacht Club. Apart from its patron, the Duke's fleet was made up largely of merchants and businessmen who kept their craft above London Bridge on the Thames. Although the fleet mainly raced on the river, members did also cruise, and one of the fleet, the *Hawke*, was chased into Calais by an American privateer in 1777 while cruising in the English Channel.

In 1815 a more aristocratic rival to the merchants' club on the Thames was formed and called "The Yacht Club" under the chairmanship of Lord Grantham. Two years later the Prince Regent, later King George IV, joined and was quickly followed by his brothers, the Duke of Clarence and the Duke of Gloucester. In 1820 when the Prince Regent became King the club became the Royal Yacht Club. In 1824 Lord Yarborough was elected as its first Commodore and took over a house on the parade at Cowes on the Isle of Wight as its clubhouse. Lord Yarborough's yacht *Falcon* weighed 366 tonnes (351 tons) and was built on the lines of a frigate of that period.

Racing was, once again, only a part of the club's activities and the early races were very rough affairs. There is a record of a race in 1829 between the *Menai*, *Lulworth* and Lord Belfast's *Louisa*, during the course of which *Louisa* and *Lulworth* collided. *Louisa*'s crew drew cutlasses and cut away part of *Lulworth*'s rigging while the two boats were entangled. Such behaviour would not meet with the approval of the racing committee nowadays. Lord Belfast owned a large number of yachts, one of which, the brig *Waterwitch*, was bought by the Admiralty in 1834. Belfast had so consistently beaten warships leaving Portsmouth in impromptu races that they wanted one of his craft as a trial horse for the British fleet. In 1829 the members of the Royal Yacht Club were given the privilege

Early 19th-century yachts prepare to start a race off Greenwich College on the River Thames in London. The cost of building yachts such as these was so high, then as now, that only the rich could afford them.

of flying the White Ensign, a British national flag when they were on board. In 1833, the yacht club became the Royal Yacht Squadron.

During the 1830s yachting expanded all over the world. It had caught on elsewhere in the long period of peace following the Napoleonic Wars. In 1831 a race was held off Tasmania, and in 1838 the Royal Hobart Regatta Association was formed. In 1844 the Royal Bermuda Yacht Club came into being. It claims to have organized the first international yacht race in 1849 between a Bermudan yacht *Pearl* and an American yacht *Brenda* with *Pearl* winning by 55 seconds.

Also in 1844 the New York Yacht Club was formed. In the United States, like Britain, yachtsmen had tended to order copies of successful commercial craft, but the American ideal was a schooner not a cutter—the Baltimore clipper. These craft, like the *Experiment*, were again used by Customs officials and smugglers.

The inevitable clash came in 1850 when Prince Albert of Britain organized the Great Exhibition, and it was suggested that an American yacht be sent over to compete in the races planned in connection with it. John Stevens, the first Commodore of the New York Yacht Club, formed a syndicate to build a yacht on the lines of the fast American pilot schooners naming her *America*.

The Falcon—*Lord Yarborough's 366-tonne yacht.*

The Duke of Cumberland's ornate tastes on land are reflected at sea in his yacht Mandamn.

She sailed across the Atlantic to beat fourteen yachts of the Royal Yacht Squadron in a race round the Isle of Wight, winning a silver cup.

Racing for this cup, since renamed the "America's Cup", has become the world's most expensive and prestigious yachting competition.

The first race was not so much a triumph of the schooner rig over the cutter rig, but of superior technology. The American boat's sails were better cut and instead of being baggy were trim and flat, allowing the boat a better performance against the wind. In the wake of *America*'s victory English yachtsmen began to sail schooners using flatter sails.

Racing had now become the *raison d'être* for yachtsmen, and those who could afford to commission and run a yacht did so to race. The cost of building and running the large boats then in vogue was so astronomic that J. P. Morgan, the American millionaire has gone down in yachting history for his remark that "if a person has to ask what a yacht will cost then he can't afford one". But the racing was unsatisfactory as a boat with a longer waterline will usually sail faster than one with a shorter waterline. So a 30 metre (100 foot) craft will always beat a 24 metre (80 foot) one. In order to even this unfair advantage out, handicap rules appeared.

A full-size replica of America, *the yacht that gave her name to the America's Cup, seen here in European waters in 1973.*

The Lulworth.

Lord Belfast's
Waterwitch, *so fast
that she was bought
by the British
Admiralty in 1834 as
a trial horse for the
British fleet.*

Mary—*a Coronation
gift from the Dutch
Government to
Charles II of Britain
in 1660.*

In 1829 the Royal Yacht Club introduced a system of handicapping with six classes divided according to tonnage. This rating, based upon a 65 kilometre (40.7 mile) race, gave Class II 0.8 kilometre (0.5 mile) advantage over Class I, the largest yachts, Class III 2 kilometres (1.25 miles), and so on until Class VI had 11 kilometres (17 miles) over Class I. This introduced an element of fairness but was not followed by every one. A lot of racing still took place as the result of a yachtsman or his club issuing a challenge laying down certain rules. A challenger would accept subject to his own rules being used. The two sides would then settle down to bargain and if a compromise was reached the race took place. As the 19th century developed, however, the rules became more comprehensive and began to guide yacht design as naval architects strove to find a way to produce boats built specifically to take advantage of the rules. Most clubs had their own rules but generally the British rules encouraged narrow deep boats and the American rules wide shallow craft. Neither set of rules led to boats built for pure seaworthiness and speed.

In 1854 an attempt was made to improve matters by the Royal Thames and Royal Mersey yacht clubs, but there was such an outcry from owners of boats built to the older rules that the Royal Thames rules were modified to produce the Thames and Royal Mersey yacht on the length of yacht and its width (beam):

$$\frac{(\text{Length} - \text{Beam}) \times \text{Beam} \times \frac{1}{2}\,\text{Beam}}{94} = \text{Tonnage}$$

This rule persists as a shorthand way of describing the true size of boats, but not measuring them for

South Coast One Design yachts. These are descendants of the first yachts to require no rating as they were functionally identical to each other.

racing. Because it penalized beam it led to "rule-cheaters", the ultimate being the famous *Oona* which had an over-all length of 14 metres (46 feet) a waterline length of 9.7 metres (32 feet) a draught of 2.44 metres (8 feet) and a beam of 1.7 metres (5.5 feet)!

In 1875 a group of yachtsmen got together to try to find a way of organizing yacht racing in Britain. There were still a number of different rules about, which did not encourage sensible association. In

1886 the first rule to ignore tonnage and hull dimensions had been formulated by Dixon Kemp:

$$\frac{\text{Waterline Length} \times \text{Sail Area}}{6000} = \text{Rating}$$

This rule was a considerable improvement over Thames Measurement as it took into account the prime factors that govern a sailing boat's speed. Some beautiful large cutters resulted from Dixon Kemp's rule, one of the finest being *Britannia*, built for the Prince of Wales, later King Edward VII. This boat was one of the most popular yachts of her time and in 1893 beat an American cutter, the *Navahoe*, in twelve out of thirteen races. In 1894 she beat *Vigilant*, another American cutter which had previously beaten Lord Dunraven's *Valkyrie II* for the America's Cup.

The days leading up to World War I were the heyday of the large racing yachts. King Edward raced his *Britannia*, Kaiser Wilhelm II of Germany had his *Meteors*, and there were *Shamrock*, *Satanita*, *Susanne*, *Bona*, and many others—all large boats needing crews of 20 or 30 to handle their enormous sail areas.

Towards the end of the 19th century a new class of yachtsman began to take to the water. Yachting had, until the 1870s, been the prerogative of the rich, but Dixon Kemp's rule allowed boats of any size to race and encouraged the building of smaller and less expensive craft. The new middle classes in Britain, Europe and America began to take an interest, and smaller racing and plain cruising boats began to appear around the coasts.

In 1903 the South Coast One Design first appeared—not the small sloop we know today, but large craft of 22 metres (73 feet). Although hardly small, they were different in that they were identical to each other and so no rating was necessary. The building of identical "class" boats had started earlier in America where it had quickly caught on, not only because it was cheaper to build a series of identical boats, but because when racing against each other the race had to be won by the more expert helmsman and crew.

In 1906 the first international attempt was made to provide a rating rule that would allow yachts of all nations to sail against each other on level handicap terms. The International Yacht Racing Union, the IYRU, was formed and from it the Metre classes. Although the United States refused to go along with the new IYRU, thirteen European nations did and ten metre classes resulted—the 5, 6, 7, 8, 9, 10, 12, 15, 19 and 23 classes. The metre classes lasted right through until after World War II, but nowadays only 6, 8 and 12 metre class boats survive, the last due entirely to the class having been chosen in 1956 for use in the America's Cup Competition. The United States eventually adopted the Metre rules in 1921, by which time the use of the Bermudan, or Marconi rig as it was often called in the early days because of the rigging required to stay the tall masts, was sweeping through the racing fleets.

In 1931 European yachtsmen adopted the American Universal Rule developed at about the same time as the Metre Rule for boats measuring over 14.5 metres (47.5 feet). This led to the building of, among other Classes, the J Class. *Shamrock V* and the two *Endeavour*s, which all fought for the America's Cup, belong to this class, as did *Valsheda*. But they were doomed by their size and cost and none survive today as racing boats.

War Baby, *a yacht typical of the 12 metre class formed in 1906 which resulted from the formation of the IYRU and which still survives as a class today.*

Vigilant *and* Valkyrie. *In 1893* Vigilant *won the America's Cup for the United States but was beaten soon afterwards by* Britannia *in a friendly race.*

Sailing becomes a popular sport

The period between the two world wars saw two developments in sailing that were not only to survive but were to grow enormously until they dominate the sailing racing scene today. These are offshore and dinghy racing.

Offshore racing could be said to have been started by three large American schooners which raced across the Atlantic in 1866. Similar races took place. In 1905 the Kaiser presented a Gold Cup to the winner of a transatlantic race. It was won by the schooner *Atlantic* with an average speed of over ten knots. In 1906 the first Bermuda Race was held, two out of the three entrants finishing. This race was revived in 1923, and in 1925 the first British offshore race of similar length was organized

Bloodhound, *winner of the 1939 Fastnet Race and subsequently skippered by H.R.H. Prince Philip of the UK until she was sold.*

—the Fastnet, won by George Martin in *Jolie Brise*. In the same year the Ocean Racing Club was founded with Martin as its Commodore and it became so popular that it was made the Royal Ocean Racing Club only six years later. The club is now responsible for the co-ordination of world-wide offshore racing along with the International Offshore Committee (IOC).

The first offshore races took place between cruising yachts but in 1926 in the Fastnet Race a new record was established by a boat specifically built for the race. She was *Hallowe'en* built by William Fife for Colonel Baxendale and she completed the race in 3 days, 19 hours and 5 minutes. The winner on corrected time was the American *Ilex*.

The Fastnet encouraged not only a new type of yacht on this side of the Atlantic but drew yachts over from the United States to compete in the race. The Americans had a more than fair share of success too. In 1928 *Nina* won handsomely. In 1931 and again in 1933 *Dorade*, designed by Olin Stephens, won. In 1935 a Stephens-designed boat, *Stormy Weather*, won from seventeen starters. The 1937 race was won by the Dutch boat *Zeearend*, and in 1939 *Bloodhound*, designed by Charles E. Nicholson, was the winner. (*Bloodhound* was bought by H.M. Queen Elizabeth II and was raced by the Royal Family until she was sold again in 1971.)

Dinghy racing had started in the 19th century, but it was not until 1927 that the very popular four metre (fourteen foot) Class was given international status. In 1928 Uffa Fox, a yachtsman and designer at Cowes, developed a V-section dinghy whose bows would lift out of the water when sailing off the wind (planing), allowing the boat to be sailed as a hydroplane. From then until the outbreak of World War II Uffa Fox dominated the International 14 Class, both as a designer and helmsman. Many other dinghy classes were developed in the years after the war, and the introduction of glass-reinforced plastics has enabled strong light hulls to be turned out in enormous numbers. Sailing is no longer the prerogative of the rich, but is within the reach of all.

CHAPTER 2

DINGHIES AND HOW TO SAIL THEM

By far the most common form of sailing craft is the dinghy. In Britain the term "dinghy" covers a wide variety of craft from the 2.5 metre (8 foot) pram dinghy powered by a simple lugsail to streamlined racing machines of 6 metres (20 feet) in length. In America a dinghy is normally a small tender attached to a larger yacht.

Small sailing craft have been in use for centuries but it was only towards the end of the 19th century with the increase in sailing for pleasure that specialized craft began to appear in classes. These were clinker-built boats.

One of the earliest of these classes was the Waterwag which first formed a class association in 1887. These 3.9 metre (13 foot) boats, fitted with a centreboard, proved to be a popular class and spread as far afield as India and Ceylon (Sri Lanka) where classes were still being raced as recently as 1960. When first built a new boat cost £15–20 ($36–48), depending upon the builder, and a set of sails cost £2–3 ($5–7) depending on whether they were made of cotton or silk!

Although small in numbers, these early dinghy classes served to spark off an interest in small-boat sailing and racing that today attracts more people in Britain as participants than the number that regularly watch association football. In various parts of the world different types and classes developed, but the first truly international yacht was the Star Class, designed by Francis Sweisguth of the United States in 1911 and sailed as a keel-boat in the Olympics until 1972.

The years after World War I saw a considerable growth of interest in dinghy sailing and the development of dinghies away from the small displacement boat concept. This breakthrough took time, and only came about because of Uffa Fox's dogged persistence. One of the fastest growing classes in the early 1920s was a development of the 4 metre (14 foot) West Country Conference dinghy. In 1927 this dinghy was given international status as the International 14.

The breakthrough came in 1928 with *Avenger* which lifted her bow up out of the water when sailed off the wind. This reduced the wetted surface of the boat and decreased the drag, thus enabling the boat to sail faster. His success was dramatic that year and out of 57 starts he achieved 52 firsts, 2 seconds and 3 thirds. The International 14 dinghy is the first of the modern dinghies, although its place has largely been taken by boats of more recent design, constructed of newer and lighter materials. There are still fleets of them to be seen in Britain, North America and New Zealand.

Racing in a General Purpose dinghy during the Welsh Harp "Little Ships" Finals in 1971. The helmsman and crew sit out to windward, to counteract the heeling force of the wind.

A typical sloop-rigged dinghy. The smaller sail is the jib and the larger the mainsail. The identification marks on the sail indicate the type of dinghy and the country of registration—in this case a Star Dinghy registered in Great Britain (K).

The first dinghy designed specifically for building at home appeared in 1931 in the United States. This was the International Snipe designed by William Crosby and sponsored by the magazine *Rudder*. Five metres (15.5 feet) long with a two-man crew, this dinghy is still one of the most popular classes in the world, a tribute to its designer. Fibreglass hulls have recently been introduced and accepted by the class association. Although not a fast planing dinghy like the International 14, the Snipe provided a more widely accepted and modern version of the earlier numerous heavier boats. It was the first of the easy-to-build class of dinghy, where a handyman could turn out within weeks a boat that could compete reasonably with one built by the professional shipwright. Inevitably this lowered prices and opened up sailing and racing to many who had been unable to afford to sail before.

The increase in dinghy sailing has been maintained by the introduction of new boat-building techniques and materials that made construction far simpler.

At first the materials were sheet plywood and water-resistant glues, largely developed for aircraft manufacture in World War II. But the basic design change that enabled the average man to build a boat at home was the *hard chine*.

Until this time many boats had been *clinker-built*, or cold-moulded to give the boat's hull a rounded shape, a process which required a fair amount of skill. In the hard chine design the boat has an angled instead of rounded cross-section and this means that the hull can basically be made up of four pieces of plywood—two on each side of the keel forming the bottom and two to make up the sides. The sides join the bottom at the chine. The plywood can be bent over considerable angles to make a fine entry at the bow but the shape squares off at about a third of the length and continues square to the transom. This sort of hull is light, inexpensive and relatively easy to construct, and once it had caught on the modern explosion in dinghy building and racing began.

Rigs and sails

Because they are relatively small and light and have small sails, dinghies can be easily handled by a crew of one or two. The sails are controlled by small ropes, *sheets* as they are called, taken directly from the corner of the sail to the hand in the case of the jib, or via a small system of blocks, often only one or two, in the case of the mainsail. It is customary for the skipper to handle the tiller and the mainsheet, and the crewman to hold on to the jib sheet. The sheets are never made fast in a dinghy but always held in the hand. This is because a sudden gust or squall can quickly tip the boat over and only by immediately releasing the sheet can a capsize be averted. In mild weather the sheets on a dinghy are frequently cleated.

The earliest dinghy sail rig was probably the lateen which was first

developed thousands of years ago in the Middle East and is still to be seen in use on dhows today. Although the rig is found all over the world, it is mainly associated with the Mediterranean, but apart from isolated instances such as the old Lowestoft Lateens in England, it was not adopted in northern Europe nor America because of the necessary length and weight of the yard, or beam, and the awkwardness of the reefing arrangements.

The lugsail was used in many early dinghies as it is easy to handle and the wind could be spilled from it quickly in a squall. It is a simple sail, copied from the many small work boats found in northern latitudes. In many respects the lugsail appears to be a development of the lateen, but it has four sides to the lateen's three. They both have spars along the top of the sail and are loose-footed which means it has no boom along the foot. But instead of the lugsail spar continuing right forward in the boat it is carried just forward of the mast and the sail is then cut straight down to its tack, or fastening, on the deck. There are two types of lugsail, the standing lug and the dipping lug. The standing lug normally has its hoisting strop fairly near the fore end of the spar

and once hoisted and its tack hardened down it is left aloft whichever sailing tack the boat is on. The dipping lug has to be changed round each time the boat tacks so that the boom is always on the leeward side of the mast. This is a clumsy procedure, entailing hauling down the front end of the spar and twisting it round the back of the mast for each tack, but if it were not done all the sail before the mast would be aback on one tack and would slow the boat up. Neither of the lugsails is seen about much these days although it is still the rig used for ships' lifeboats.

The gaff rig is another old favourite, and although not used in modern racing dinghies it is still to be seen on a few dinghies. Like the lugsail the sail is four-sided, but the spar does not extend forward of the mast. Instead it has a jaw that fits round it. The luff, or forward edge, of the sail is secured round the mast and the sail's foot may run on the boom, like other sails, besides being laced or loose-footed.

The gunter rig is a cross between the gaff and the Bermudan. The simplest way to think of it is as a gaff rig with the spar hoisted up vertically so that it acts as an extension to the mast. The sail is basically

Above left: a typical clinker-built dinghy. The planks overlap those below and are fastened with clinched nails.

Above: an International Canoe.

A felucca with a lateen sail, first developed by the Arabs thousands of years ago.

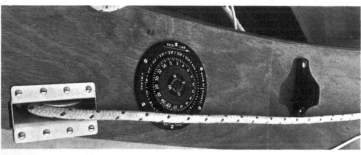

The starboard side of a Flying Dutchman showing the jib sheet arrangement and compass.

to prevent the mast toppling forward. In most dinghies, however, the pull of the mainsheet on the mainsail provides almost sufficient support for the mast and no backstay is carried. Instead, the shrouds come down to the sides, behind the mast, so that they combine side support with a small amount of bracing aft.

The headsail, or jib, is hanked on to the forestay. Along its leading edge, or luff, are small clips called *hanks* that hold the sail on to the stay. The sail is hoisted by means of a rope called the *jib halyard* which runs through a pulley at the masthead. The halyard is hauled up tight as slackness in the luff of the sail causes bagging which reduces the sail's efficiency. To stop the sail rising too high and to provide a hold, or tack, at the bottom end of the luff the tack is shackled on to a deck fitting which also acts as a base for the forestay. The other two sides of the sail are called the *leach* and the *foot* and the point of the sail where they meet is normally reinforced to stand up to strain.

Two sheets are fitted to the clew (corner) of the jib and one is led to each side of the boat through a deck fitting. The down-wind or leeward sheet is used when sailing and the windward sheet is left slack to be recovered and hauled in when the boat goes about, when it becomes the leeward sheet. The placing of the deck fitting, or lead (leed), is important. If it is too far forward the foot of the sail will be too slack, if too far aft the leach will be slack. As good a way as any of finding a position for the lead is to draw an imaginary line through the clew, perpendicular to the forestay. Where this line reaches the deck, fasten the lead. It may want adjustment later though, once the sail has had some use and the cloth has stretched.

triangular and usually a small jib is carried. Although the gunter rig is still used, it has been largely displaced by simpler more efficient rigs.

The development of dinghy rigs has largely settled on to the Bermudan rig. A small light-weight mast of wood or aluminium is set, or stepped, in the front part of the boat and supported by three wires, or *stays*. One stay holds the mast forward and prevents the weight of the wind in the sails breaking the mast back. This is called the *forestay*. On each side of the mast are two other stays which prevent the mast toppling over sideways. These are the *shrouds*. In some cases a further stay, the *backstay*, is rigged from the masthead to the stern, in order

The mainsail, sometimes—particularly in smaller and single-handed dinghies—the only sail, has its luff attached to the rear side of the mast. Originally it was attached by means of lacing which ran round the mast and through eyelets in the luff. Nowadays it is more commonly held firmly into a slot in the rear of the mast by a bolt rope sewn on the luff side of the sail. In many cases, though, a track is fitted on to the mast, into which the reinforced luff can be slid. The mainsail is hoisted by means of another rope, also led through the masthead and back to the deck, called the *main halyard*.

The foot of the mainsail is attached to a horizontal length of aluminium or wood called a *boom*. At the mast end of the boom where the sail's tack is fastened, the boom is connected to the mast by means of a fitting called a *gooseneck*, a universal joint. The gooseneck's purpose is to allow the boom to move sideways and upwards at the same time.

The tack of the mainsail is fastened to the boom and to adjust the tension in the luff of the sail the gooseneck is hauled downwards on a small track on the mast. This has another purpose as the helmsman will want to adjust the luff, tightening it to flatten the sail, as when going to windward in a good breeze, and slackening the luff to put more full-ness into the sail as when running or in a light wind. In some dinghies the gooseneck is fixed on to the mast so that it cannot be slid up or down. The mainsail, therefore, has another *cringle* (the name given to the brass circular fitting in the sail which takes the strain and wear at attachment points) a few inches above the tack. This is known as the *Cunningham hole*. It provides a means of tightening the luff by allowing a short length of rope to be led from the deck, through the hole and back.

The mainsheet is attached to the outer end of the boom where the sail is made fast. The sheet, usually a tackle, is fastened on to a *horse*. This is the name given to the bar along which the sheet block slides. The bar runs over the tiller thus avoiding interference between the two. In some boats, where the tiller and the mainsheet are so close as to tangle up, the mainsheet block slides in a track.

Since a sailing boat is powered by the pressure of the wind on the sail, the stronger the wind the less sail will be required to provide the same driving force. Unnecessary pressure on the sails will not increase the boat's speed, but will put extra

This sailing lifeboat has the standing lugsail rig widely used in early dinghies.

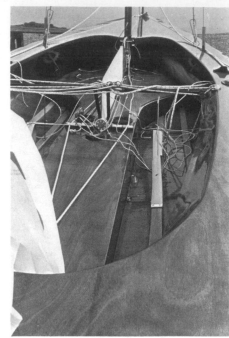

strain on the mast and rigging and increase the chances of a capsize. Reducing the sail in size is called *reefing*.

There are two basic ways of reefing—slab and roller. Slab reefing is where a section of sail above the foot is hauled down to cringles in the luff and leach of the sail which become the new tack and clew respectively. On a straight line drawn between these two cringles a number of brass eyelets are set in the sail so that when the new tack and clew are hauled down into place the eyelets are just above the boom. These eyelets are called *reefing points*, and short lengths of line are run through them and round the boom and then tied down firmly with a reef knot. In this way the whole of the new foot of the sail is fastened to the boom evenly and the reduced sail will set properly. In larger boats two or three lines of reefing points are often found to give a choice of sail areas.

In roller reefing a ratchet at the gooseneck is used to roll up the sail by revolving the boom. The ratchet stops the boom rolling when the wind fills the sail. Roller reefing is quicker and easier to operate, but unless the boom is properly shaped the sail loses shape as it is rolled up. Slab reefing is therefore favoured, especially by the racing fraternity.

The centreboard

Such light shallow-draught boats as dinghies, where there is little hull beneath the water, would quickly be blown down wind unless some additional form of lateral resistance is provided. This is achieved by means of a centreboard. In most dinghies the centreboard takes the form of a dagger-shaped piece of wood, often weighted at the bottom end, which is pulled up and lowered by means of a pulley in a narrow watertight box built longitudinally down the keel. The centreboard passes through a carved slot in the keel. When beating to weather, that is trying to sail as near as possible to the direction from which the wind is blowing, considerable grip on the water is required and the centreboard is fully lowered. When running dead down wind the resistance of the hull is made minimal by raising the centreboard.

A helmsman soon learns exactly how much centreboard to use in varying conditions and to balance the amount of lateral resistance required with the need to keep no more centreboard down below the hull than necessary as it increases the resistance to the boat's movement through the water.

Nearly all dinghies are steered by operating a *tiller* connected to a *rudder* slung over the transom. The rudder hangs below the bottom of the boat to give a good grip in the water. In some dinghies the rudder is made in two parts so that the lower half is hinged and can be raised or lowered depending on how much grip is required, just like the centreboard. Because dinghies are light, the helmsman and crew have to sit out on the windward side to provide a balance for the weight of wind in the sail and stop the boat turning over. In order that the helmsman can get his weight out and still steer, a hinged tiller extension is fitted to allow him to steer.

Nowadays, in order to balance the greater sail area and lighter weight of modern dinghies, compared to dinghies of 50 years ago, the crewman is often put out on a trapeze to provide greater righting moment.

Rigging a hinged dinghy rudder.

Many types of small dinghies can be launched directly into the surf because of their lack of depth underwater.

Spinnakers

Opposite: A typical Fireball dinghy sailing under its spinnaker. The main difficulty in setting a spinnaker is caused by the fact that none of its sides is attached to a stay or spar. Instead it is linked to the mast by a boom and controlled by halyards, one from the boom, the other from the sail.

A group of racing yachts approach the marker buoy sporting a colourful array of spinnakers.

In many classes of dinghy, *spinnakers* are carried to provide extra pull when running or broad reaching (i.e. when the wind is blowing from the quarter and not from the beam or from right astern), and when the wind is forward of the beam. Whereas most dinghy sails nowadays are Terylene or Dacron, spinnakers are made of very light nylon usually in bright colours.

The spinnaker is a difficult sail to handle, as unlike the jib and mainsail it does not have any of its three sides attached along its length to a stay or spar. Instead it is held in position by a halyard up the mast and its tack is attached to a guy held out by a spinnaker boom or pole. The pole is attached to the forward edge of the mast and holds the tack of the sail well out. The modern balloon-type spinnaker is best set high, so to support the pole a topping lift and down-haul are fitted to steady it. The topping lift leads from higher up the mast to the

outer end of the pole or to the balance-point half-way along it to hold the pole up and the down-haul does the same thing downwards. It is important to keep the spinnaker pole horizontal as this keeps the spinnaker out as far as possible.

The clew of the spinnaker is attached to a sheet which is played, or eased in or out, to get the maximum pull out of the sail. As a rough guide, the spinnaker pole should be perpendicular to the wind direction and then the sheet should be let out as much as possible, just so the luff of the sail curls in every few seconds. If the spinnaker luffs, or curls over too much so that the whole sail starts to fill in, the sail can be reset by hauling in on the sheet. If the sail has luffed too far for hauling in the sheet to stop it, the helmsman has no choice but to head the boat further off away down wind until the spinnaker fills again.

Spinnakers are not difficult sails to handle provided that everything has been thought out and prepared in advance. First one has to decide

which tack the boat is going to be on and then put the pole out on the new windward side. Then the sail must be got ready to hoist with its halyard, guy and sheet clipped on. It is usual to hoist the spinnaker on the lee side, sheltered by the jib, so the guy has to be run round outside the forestay before hoisting. It will be hardened in as soon as the sail has been hoisted and the halyard cleated.

There are many different ways of hoisting a spinnaker, but one very good method is to keep the sail in a plastic bucket with the head, tack and clew on top. When the time comes to set the sail it is a simple matter to clip the halyard, sheet and guy on and then hoist. In some boats, a special chute is fitted into the foredeck and the spinnaker is stuffed into this. The Flying Dutchman has this arrangement. This has been further improved recently so that the spinnaker can be hauled down straight into the chute by means of a line attached to the centre of the sail and lead down through a hole in the bottom of the chute into the cockpit. This has the added advantage of allowing the spinnaker to be quickly handled and stowed and saves vital seconds at the end of a run. The sail is also ready for hoisting again immediately.

Safety

A word about safety in a dinghy or any boat will not be amiss as it can never be over-emphasized. The neglect of any of the basic principles will not only endanger the sailor's life but also the lives of those dedicated to life-saving. Near-by yachtsmen and members of life-saving organizations will all put their own lives at risk to save a person in distress in the water. It

In the event of a capsize the procedure to be followed to right the boat is shown here. Do not panic. Even if the boat cannot be righted help should not be !ong in coming so long as someone ashore has been advised of the day's sailing programme.

is a moral crime to put other people's lives at risk through sheer stupidity.

If you get into trouble see if you cannot get out of it before calling for help. Refloating after going aground is simple enough as you can probably push yourself off, but check the bottom first, it may be deep mud in which case you must go warily.

Perhaps the most tricky situation occurs if the boat capsizes. As soon as it seems inevitable, ensure that your lifejacket is inflated (unless it is the type filled with buoyant material). Next swim round and let go the sheets and the sail halyards. If you can get the sails down so much the better as they will be under water and will act as a drag when you come to right the boat. Lower the centreboard to its fullest extent if it was not already right down and then swim round to the other side of the boat. The boat will, with any luck, be lying on its side still so grab hold of the centreboard and start to pull down by climbing on to it. Put your hands on the gunwale and with your feet on the centreboard, lean back. Your weight should slowly bring the boat upright. As soon as the boat is on an even keel again let go and clamber aboard. If the water is deep enough the boat may have turned right upside down. In that case let go the sheets and then try to bring the boat upright by climbing up one of the upturned sides. It is not always easy and takes time.

Once the boat is upright get the bow round head to sea and bale out. Even if you have self-balers take the worst of the water out before starting to sail again.

If for any reason you cannot get the boat upright again, stay with it unless you can walk ashore. The reason for this is that an upturned boat is more noticeable than a swimmer and it is the first place a rescue craft will look for you. Also as nearly all dinghies have buoyancy of some sort, the boat will support you, and rescue should not be too long in arriving, especially if you are in a race. If you are just going out for a sail on your own, make sure that someone knows where you have gone. They can raise the alarm if you are not back when expected.

Most dinghy sailors have capsized at one time or another and the speed with which one can right a dinghy and get sailing again can make all the difference in a race. In the 1971 British Finn Championships, for instance, Ian MacDonald-Smith capsized, righted himself and went on to win the race and the championship. This sort of speed is the result of practice as much as anything else. It is a good idea to go out in a dinghy with your skipper or crew and deliberately capsize in water that you can both stand up in and then practise getting the boat upright again. Ideally, though, check the weather forecast and choose a warm sunny day for it!

Another potentially dangerous situation occurs when one of the crew falls overside into the water. The person's lifejacket should keep him afloat but the other crew members must immediately luff the boat up into the wind and either sail back to the person in the water or allow the wind to drift the boat back. Once close, any piece of rope can be thrown and the person hauled in. If you can't get the person aboard, tie a bowline round his chest and ensure that he is held close-to while you sail the boat to the nearest shallow water and then pull him aboard.

Once again, man overboard drill should be practised frequently, and both members of the crew should

Choosing a dinghy

Most people start off sailing either as crew in someone else's dinghy or at a sailing school. It is obviously better to learn as much as possible about a boat before investing in one, as apart from learning which type of dinghy interests you, you will learn what to look for when buying one.

When choosing a racing dinghy, you have to decide whether to buy a boat in a one-design or a development class. Generally speaking, in a one-design class every boat built over the years will be exactly the same and conform to the plans drawn up by the designer. Every boat will not only look the same, but can be expected to handle the same as every other boat in the class. The advantage of this is that older boats can compete on fairly level terms with more recently built boats. In a popular one-design class such as the Enterprise, boats maintain a relatively high second-hand value.

In a development class, such as the International 14 dinghy, individual designers are allowed a free hand within certain limits to change the hull shape and the layout of the boat. New ideas are encouraged, and the whole class is constantly developing with faster and faster boats being produced. Normally the development classes attract experts who bring their experience to play when building a new boat. Competition is not just restricted to the crew's skill but also includes technical knowhow, and boats rapidly become outdated. Class leaders will probably build a new boat every year or two so old boats will change hands comparatively cheaply; but they are likely to be outclassed in competition.

It is possible to build a boat very

GP dinghies racing in the "Little Ships" finals. The races were sponsored by a leading British paint manufacturer who had hoped to organize a world championship. The response from non-European countries was not sufficient for this, however, and the IYRU refused to recognize the event as such. The event was changed to an Open European championship with teams from ten European countries and one from New Zealand competing for the title. The UK team won the competition.

be able to sail the boat single-handed back on to a lifejacket thrown into the water. As you will have realized, the ability to swim is an essential part of your personal safety measures and no one should be allowed to go out in a dinghy unless they can swim fully clothed and wearing a lifejacket. It is equally important to check your boat before sailing and see that all your gear is in good shape and, in particular, that all equipment is on board. It is very easy to forget to check that items such as the baler, a knife, paddles, and so on are all in the boat when launching from a trailer on a crowded slipway. In the first hectic moments after launching, when the sheets are being trimmed, the centre-board adjusted and the helmsman and crew settling down, there are other things to think about and you may not notice you have forgotten something until it is too late.

simply at home, either directly from plans or from a kit. *In either case follow the instructions closely* and if you are in doubt seek advice. If the performance of your boat is to be the same as others of similar design and is perhaps to race against them, it must be identical. There is always a tendency to think one can improve a design—forget it. Unless you are a dinghy-designer, the improvements you think you are incorporating into the boat would have been included by the designer or class.

Just one word of warning, do not try and save money by using anything but marine plywood, water-resistant glue and brass, copper or stainless-steel fastenings. You will cut the life of your boat by two-thirds.

With the development of the sport dinghy clubs have grown up on almost every stretch of water suitable for sailing, from reservoirs to the sea. In America, clubs allow almost any dinghy, but many British clubs now choose one or two classes to provide level competitive racing. Consequently, when you are deciding which dinghy you want to choose in Britain, check which classes are sailed near your home.

Dinghies can, from an organizational point of view, be divided into three types. One-offs, or small classes which are sailed locally by clubs or individuals, make up the largest in numbers. If a dinghy proves popular and spreads farther afield, the class association can apply to the national sailing authority, in Britain this is the Royal Yachting Association, for the class to be recognized as a National Class. These could well include local craft particularly suited to one country which might not suit another. The third group is the International Classes, officially designated as such by the International Yacht Racing Union, for which world championships are arranged, usually every two years.

Building a Cherub dinghy at home.

Some international dinghy classes

Optimist
LOA 4.00 m. 13.17 ft.
Beam 1.13 m. 3.7 ft.
Draught 0.08 m. 0.25 ft.
Draught (c/b down) 0.71 m.
2.33 ft..
Sail area 3.25 sq. m.
35 sq. ft.
Weight 35 kilos. 77 lb.

Cadet
LOA 3.22 m. 10.56 ft.
Beam 1.27 m. 4.16 ft.
Draught 0.23 m. 0.75 ft.
Draught (c/b down) 0.76 m.
2.5 ft.
Sail area 5.16 sq. m.
55.5 sq. ft.
Spinnaker 4.65 sq. m.
50 sq. ft.
Weight 54.43 kilos. 120 lb.

OK
LOA 4.00 m. 13.17 ft.
Beam 1.42 m. 4.66 ft.
Draught 0.18 m. 0.58 ft.
Draught (c/b down) 0.94 m.
3.08 ft.
Sail area 8.36 sq. m.
90 sq. ft.
Weight 72 kilos. 159 lb.

420
LOA 4.19 m. 13.75 ft.
Beam 1.69 m. 5.42 ft.
Draught 0.15 m. 0.5 ft.
Draught (c/b down) 1.06 m.
3.5 ft.
Sail area 10.23 sq. m.
110 sq. ft.
Spinnaker 10.01 m. 97 sq. ft.
Weight 99.79 kilos. 220 lb.

International 14
LOA 4.27 m. 14 ft.
Beam 1.42–1.69 m.
4.66–5.5 ft.
Draught unrestricted
Sail area 11.61 sq. m.
125 sq. ft.
Spinnaker unlimited
Weight 102.05 kilos 225 lb.

Enterprise
LOA 4.04 m. 13.25 ft.
Beam 1.62 m. 5.25 ft.
Draught 0.18 m. 0.58 ft.
Draught (c/b down) 0.96 m.
3.17 ft.
Sail area (cruising)
7.43 sq. m. 80 sq. ft.
Sail area (racing)
10.50 sq. m. 113 sq. ft.
Weight 90.26 kilos. 199 lb.

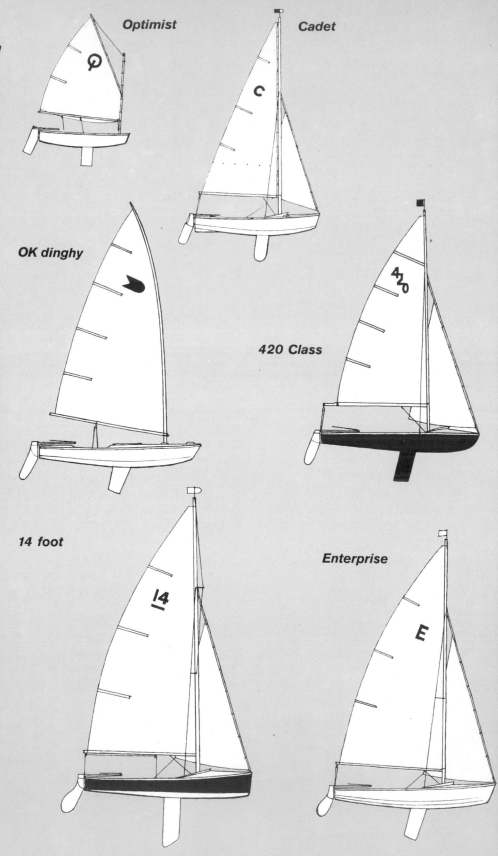

Optimist

Cadet

OK dinghy

420 Class

14 foot

Enterprise

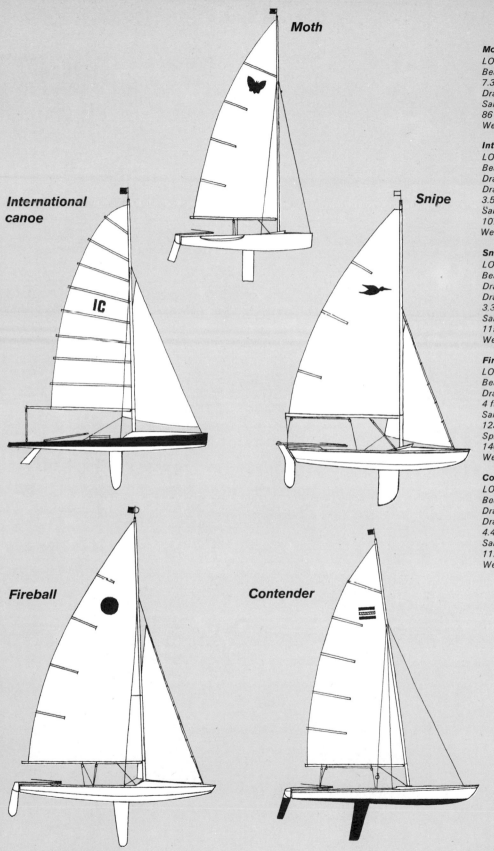

Moth

Moth
LOA 3.34 m. 11 ft.
Beam (maximum) 2.25 m.
7.33 ft.
Draught unrestricted
Sail area 8.00 sq. m.
86 sq. ft.
Weight unrestricted

International Canoe
LOA 5.20 m. 17.06 ft.
Beam 1.02 m. 3.35 ft.
Draught 0.08 m. 0.25 ft.
Draught (c/b down) 1.06 m.
3.5 ft.
Sail area 10.00 sq. m.
107.64 sq. ft.
Weight 63 kilos. 137 lb.

Snipe
LOA 4.72 m. 15.5 ft.
Beam 1.54 m. 5 ft.
Draught 0.18 m. 0.58 ft.
Draught (c/b down) 1.03 m.
3.37 ft.
Sail area 10.70 sq. m.
115 sq. ft.
Weight 172.82 kilos. 381 lb.

Fireball
LOA 4.93 m. 16.17 ft.
Beam 1.37 m. 4.5 ft.
Draught (c/b down) 1.22 m.
4 ft.
Sail area 11.43 sq. m.
123 sq. ft.
Spinnaker 13.01 sq. m.
140 sq. ft.
Weight 79.38 kilos. 175 lb.

Contender
LOA 4.88 m. 16 ft.
Beam 1.43 m. 4.66 ft.
Draught 0.14 m. 0.48 ft.
Draught (c/b down) 1.36 m.
4.45 ft.
Sail area 10.41 sq. m.
112 sq. ft.
Weight 104.33 kilos 230 lb.

International canoe

Snipe

Fireball

Contender

CHAPTER 3

MULTIHULLS AND
EXPERIMENTAL CRAFT

Multihulls, as the name suggests, are boats with more than one hull. The principles of construction are based upon lightness and the old techniques of boat-building only partly apply. Many people consider that the multihull is suited to amateur construction and has until very recently been largely ignored by traditional boat-builders. As a result the multihull followers have been distinctive for their enthusiasm and their willingness to experiment. Traditionally the boats built for use in Europe and North America were heavy monohulls, relying upon internal ballast to provide weight to balance the force of the wind on the sails and keep the boat upright. The small boats and dinghies relied upon the crew sitting out on the gunwale of the boat to keep it from capsizing. As design and building techniques improved, the ballast was formed into a streamlined keel beneath the boat, which, by increasing the distance of the weight below the centre of gravity of the boat, increased the righting moment to provide an even greater stability. In fact, it was found that by putting the boat's ballast in the keel instead of in the bilges inside the boat, the amount of ballast could be greatly reduced, and the boat would be lighter as a result and so could be sailed faster. The boat still depended for its stability on having a weighted keel, however, and if the stability could be provided by other means a lighter and faster boat would result.

The solution to this problem had already been found in the South Pacific where for centuries the Polynesians, whose shipbuilding had been limited in size by the materials available, had doubled their capacity for ocean passages by lashing two hulls alongside each other. The wider platform this created effectively gave sufficient stability to

Opposite: A Polynesian-style catamaran — Ladyline. Launched by Princess Margaret in the late 1960s, the boat was wrecked off Minorca in 1975.

Financial Times —a fast trimaran but unsuccessful in the 1974 Round Britain Race.

balance the sail without using ballast. These boats covered incredible distances at sea, and the Polynesians spread throughout the whole South Pacific islands in them. Simpler versions, called *proas*, had been developed where the mast was rigged in one hull and another, usually smaller, hull was rigged alongside as an outrigger. The proas could only sail by keeping the outrigger to leeward of the main hull. This meant that when they tacked about they had to reverse direction. They compensated for not carrying ballast by "leaning" on the outrigger.

The first modern multihull was designed in America by Nathaniel Herreshof before the turn of the century. His 9 metre (30 foot) catamaran was so successful that it was banned from racing, and it was not until well into the 20th century that interest in multihulls arose again.

Development has been in three basic types—the *catamaran*, a twin-hulled vessel similar to the Polynesian ocean-going craft which has the mast stepped midway between the hulls; the *proa*, working on exactly the same principles as the South Pacific variety, and a development of the proa called a *trimaran* which has outriggers on both sides and so does not have to reverse direction when it goes about.

In all these three styles of boat the ballast has been done away with so that the finished craft weighs just more than half of the equivalent length monohull boat. The performance of these multihulls hard on the wind has not been a particular improvement on the monohull. Despite the fitting of light-weight keels to provide a grip in the water,

Below: an unusual feature of the trimaran Swingalong *is the collapsible outer hull.*

Below right: a catamaran can sail faster than the speed of the wind behind her, as illustrated in this diagram. A, the boat is sailing at non-planing speed. At B the craft with its bow lifted out of the water planes on its own bow wave— running away from the sea wave.

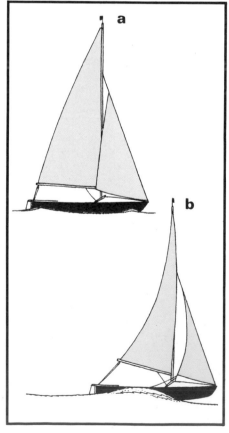

the weight of a monohull carries it through a wave better. Off the wind, however, the multihulls are very much faster, due to hull shape and absence of ballast.

Construction techniques in boat-building in recent years have been changed and improved by the introduction of first plywood and later glass-reinforced plastics. Both these methods of building have enabled shipyards to build lighter and stronger boats and these advantages have particularly favoured the multi-hull designs where the basic principle is lightness upon which results depend.

A different sort of sailing

Sailing a catamaran (cat) differs from a monohull in that the cat, being so much lighter, goes a lot faster and so relative to the craft,

the wind comes round much more than in a dinghy. In order to get the best out of a cat, once the boat starts to gather speed, the helmsman veers away slightly more which effectively increases the strength of the relative wind and allows a further increase in speed. It is quite possible for a catamaran close hauled to be going down wind faster than the true wind as the diagram on page 36 indicates.

Once the trick of sailing a small light-weight racing catamaran has been mastered, the result is perhaps more rewarding than in any other form of sailing. In craft such as the *Tornado* or *Hobie Cat* the acceleration is dramatic, not surprising when one considers that a Tornado weighs only 204 kg (450 lb) and a Hobie Cat only 159 kg (350 lb) and both boats set more sail and are lighter than many ocean-going craft

An Olympic-class Tornado catamaran flying a hull. The crew is harnessed and standing out on the weather hull.

Leaning as far out as possible, the helmsman has to use a tiller extension to enable him to steer with his left hand while controlling the main sheet with his right.

If the crew are slow getting out to windward of the boat as it gathers speed, a capsize is inevitable, unless the sheets are immediately let go, or the boat luffed up into the wind.

Once the crew are out to windward, in the right strength of wind, their weight will lift the windward hull right out of the water so that the boat is sailing along on only one hull, rather like a stunt car being driven on two wheels. The windward hull can lift well clear and the helmsman has to watch the balance carefully as it is at this stage that an extra gust can blow the boat right over. Another danger is that of submerging the bow of the leeward hull. To avoid this the crewman moves crabwise towards the stern of the boat to lift the bow. If he is not quick enough the leeward bow will dig in and the boat will start to somersault. The boat can cartwheel through the air along the surface of the water, throwing out the helmsman and hopefully, if his trapeze unhooks, the crewman as well. Otherwise he will be dragged along until the boat stops. Even if the boat does not somersault when the bow digs in, the crewman will probably lose his footing and his momentum will carry him straight out over the bow suspended by the trapeze wire. The crewman has now become a human pendulum and having gone out as far as the wire allows he will swing back. If the helmsman is not quick at throwing himself flat, he will be knocked straight over the stern into the water by the crewman.

At the other extreme, if the boat has one hull flying and the wind suddenly dies, the crewman will be dropped into water as the windward hull comes back down. He can only prevent this if he can swing himself aboard on to the light nylon trampoline that is stretched between the

of equal length. As the cat gathers speed, the crewman has to clip himself on to the trapeze. The trapeze consists of a canvas harness wrapped round the lower half of the body with straps running between the legs and over the shoulders. In the centre is a stainless-steel hook that clips on to a wire suspended from the masthead. Once the crewman is clipped on, he throws himself out so that he is hanging full length over the windward side of the boat in order to prevent the windward hull flying right up, thus preventing a capsize. His only support is the trapeze and he holds himself in place with rubber-soled shoes on the gunwale of the boat. While perched out like this he may also have control of the jib sheet. The helmsman has a long tiller extension so that he too can get his weight as far out as possible to help the balance and still steer the boat. The helmsman also controls the main sheet, which will be held in his free hand so that he can let it go quickly if necessary. Sailing a cat like this is exhilarating and demands considerable physical fitness, stamina and very quick reflexes.

Opposite: Unicorn class catamarans prepare to launch off the beach.

two hulls and acts as the working platform.

The only time a cat seems slower and safer than a racing dinghy is when tacking. The helmsman brings the bow up into the wind and releases the main sheet so that the mainsail flaps. The crewman swings inboard on his trapeze, unclips, and dives across the boat hauling in the other jib sheet as he goes. Because of its light weight a catamaran has less momentum than a dinghy, does not carry through the wind as quickly, and so there is more time to get set on the other tack. Once the boat is round, however, the crewman must clip on his trapeze and throw himself out again pretty quickly.

The Tornado is one of the lightest and fastest multihulls as it is designed for racing. By far the majority of catamarans and trimarans are designed for cruising and as such carry a lot of extra weight which causes a loss of speed. Some very long voyages have been made in multihulls, the best known being David Lewis sailing round the world with his family in 1964–67 in his catamaran *Rehu Moana* (see page 58), Lieutenant-Commander Nigel Tetley's almost completed single-handed non-stop circumnavigation in 1968–69 in his trimaran *Victress* which broke up off the Azores with only 1,600 kilometres (1,000 miles) to go (see page 122) and Alain Colas in his trimaran *Manureva* (ex-*Pen Duick IV*) in which he made a solo circumnavigation in 1973–74 stopping only in Australia. During this voyage Colas became the first single-handed sailor to sail 6,400 kilometres (4,000 miles) in twenty days, an average speed of over 8 knots.

Because of their stability, multihulls make attractive cruising boats and properly handled there is little danger of a capsize. While they don't bash through the waves to windward, they sail almost upright on a less fine course and they quickly outpace a similar size monohull off the wind. An indication of the increasing popularity of multihulls is the number of production cruisers now available on the market, and, of course, the acceptance of the Tornado as an Olympic Class.

Multihull races

The first major international multihull competition came about as a result of a challenge issued to the Americans by the Chapman Sands Sailing Club of Essex in Britain. In 1961 the Americans responded and presented the International Catamaran Challenge Cup for a competition for C Class catamarans. This

Before a catamaran is built, models are made to enable the owners and designers to study how the craft will react to various weather conditions. Here Robin Knox-Johnston and Gerry Boxall examine a model of British Oxygen *in which they won the 1974 Round Britain Race.*

class was recognized by the IYRU which laid down that the boats were not to exceed 7.6 metres (25 feet) in length and 4.3 metres (14 feet) in breadth. The first series was won by Britain which went on to defend the cup successfully seven times. The trophy was eventually given the name of "The Little America's Cup". Although far smaller than an America's Cup contender and limited to a crew of two, the C Class cats can achieve far higher speeds and have been logged at over 30 knots. In 1969 Britain lost the cup to Denmark who in turn the following year lost it to Australia. The Australians held the cup in 1974 with *Miss Nylex*, beating off a New Zealand challenge. This cat does not have a sail as such, but a large aerofoil complete with trim tab

proved increasingly attractive to European multihull enthusiasts. Until such time as the IYRU can provide a system of rating multihulls to the International Offshore Rule, they will not be brought together with monohulls for competitive racing. Currently, very few races exist which are open to both types of boat, and in these cases a rule-of-thumb system of handicapping has to be used. The best example of this is the four-yearly single-handed transatlantic race from Plymouth in Britain to Newport, Rhode Island, in the United States. This race is open to any boat above 7 metres (24 feet) which is seaworthy in the opinion of the organizers, the Royal Western Yacht Club of England. The race has encouraged the building of many experimental types of

Financial Times under trial in 1974.

that resembles a Jumbo jet's tail-plane more than anything else.

Although multihull racing has not yet reached the level of support and organization found in the mono-hull offshore racing field, races specifically for multihulls are increasing in numbers. In Europe, the best-known race is the 304 kilo-metre (190 mile) Crystal Trophy, sailed from Cowes in the Isle of Wight to Cherbourg in France and finishing at Plymouth. This race was started in the 1960s and has

boat. Multihulls in particular have benefited and the fourth of these races was won by a French trimaran *Pen Duick IV*, sailed by Alain Colas, from an entry of over 50 boats, a third of which were multihulls. His time was a record for the race. One of the attractions in this race is the choice of routes. If one goes the shortest distance across the northern part of the Atlantic, head winds will be encountered which would normally favour the mono-hull. The alternative is to go south

Three Cheers, *second in the 1974 Round Britain Race, was lost at sea during the 1976 OSTAR.*

To bring this graceful racing catamaran from the model pictured on page 40 to this standard of finish took time, money and above all love of racing at sea.

to the latitude of the Azores in which case following winds are more likely, which would appear to favour the multihulls.

Another race, also organized by the Royal Western Yacht Club that is open to all types of boat, is the Round Britain Race. This race, for a crew of two, is also held every four years and has provided an interesting comparison between the two types of boat. The first race held in 1966 was a multihull walk-over and was won convincingly by *Toria*, a trimaran.

The small crew has to be constantly alert to avoid shipping, and as the yachts are seldom far from land, navigation is important. The race has been divided into five legs—Plymouth in Devon to Cork in Eire, Cork to Barra in the Outer Hebrides, Barra to Lerwick in the Shetland Isles, Lerwick to Lowestoft in East Anglia and Lowestoft back to Plymouth. Each boat must stop exactly 48 hours in each of the four staging points, which provides an opportunity for the crews to rest and make any necessary repairs.

In the 1970 race, monohulls won both the open and handicap prizes, but not without a struggle. An American, Phil Weld in *Trumpeter*, a very fast Kelsall-designed-and-built trimaran, was putting up a good race for the open prize when his boat sustained damage which lost valuable time for repairs. On the last leg an Apache Class catamaran looked like making a fight for line honours, when it overturned off the Isle of Wight. In fact the open winner of the race, by over two days, was *Ocean Spirit*, owned and sailed jointly by Robin Knox-Johnston and Leslie Williams. The Handicap prize went to Captain Mike McMullen in his sloop *Binkie* which he and his crew rowed the last 29 kilometres (18 miles) in a flat calm to clinch their winning position.

These races have undoubtedly encouraged multihull development and for the 1974 Round Britain Race a number of new multihulls were developed. The largest was the 21.3 metres (70 foot) long 9.8 metres (32 foot) wide catamaran designed by Rod Macalpine-Downie called *British Oxygen*. This boat, sailed by Robin Knox-Johnston and Gerry Boxall, is the largest racing cat yet built and indicates that the limit to the actual size of these boats has not yet been reached. Although resembling a grown-up Tornado in many respects, she has a crew of only two to cope with a sail area as great as an America's Cup yacht. Because of her large size, a relatively greater wind force is required to drive the boat to its maximum speed, but nevertheless 26 knots has been achieved in a Force 7 wind.

In the 1974 race the first places went to multihull-owners. *British Oxygen* was the winner by the narrow margin of 71 minutes from Mike McMullen in *Three Cheers*, a very fast trimaran designed by the American Dick Newisk, who also designed the third boat to finish, Phil Weld's 18.3 metre (60 foot) trimaran *Gulf Streamer*. Fourth home was Alain Colas in *Manureva*. Even a 10.7 metres (35 foot) trimaran *Three Legs of Mann* came in before the first monohull to finish, Leslie Williams's 24.4 metres (80 foot) ketch *Burton Cutter*. The 1974 race took place in an unusually windy July with head winds the norm for the course. Despite these conditions, which traditionally have been thought to favour the heavier monohulls, the race showed that a well-designed and well-crewed multihull was more than capable of sailing as fast as a keel boat to windward, and would produce much faster speeds the moment a reach or run was possible.

Hydrofoils

Perhaps the most interesting introduction recently has been hydrofoils. Hydrofoils, or "wings" underneath a boat which lift the hull up out of the water once the boat gathers speed, are a fairly recent innovation for power boats where engines can provide the speed necessary to give the required lift. Once the boat is moving fast enough the hydrofoils lift the hull up clear of the water and the boat skims the surface on these "wings". As the hydrofoils have very little wetted surface, speeds of up to 60 or 70 knots can be achieved with a hull and engines that would normally only achieve 20 or so knots if the whole hull rested in the water.

Ocean Spirit, *winner by over two days of the 1970 Round Britain Race.*

Opposite above:
Hugh Murray—
director of Planesail
—seen here with the
part-completed
structure of Nova 2.
Planesail was an
interesting experiment
in using vertical
aerofoils instead of
sails but it was
scrapped because of
lack of capital.

Opposite centre:
Mayfly, an A-class
catamaran which has
been fitted with
hydrofoils to lift the
hull out of the water
in order to reduce the
wetted surface.

Opposite below:
Crossbow reaches a
speed of 31.09 knots.
The crew are in the
crewpod which also
contains winches
used to balance the
boat.
Crossbow II has now
recorded a speed of
31.8 knots.

Once hulls could be made light and stable enough, hydrofoils were a logical next step, and for nearly twenty years yachtsmen on both sides of the Atlantic have tried to produce a really effective sailing hydrofoil. So far the results have been mixed, the main problem being to achieve the exact shape of hydrofoil to provide the lift required.

Once moving on the foils, other problems arise, the major one being to manœuvre. When tacking, the boat loses speed and drops back into the water again. If gybing, the sudden change in direction of the force being applied to the boat by the sails from one side to another can easily cause a capsize as the weight on the hydrofoils changes. No one has yet come up with the solution to these problems, but some interesting experiments have been made, and the development is at a stage when anyone without benefit of expensive testing facilities could come up with a breakthrough. This is, perhaps, the attraction.

Since the early Baker hydrofoil sailing craft built in America in the 1950s, much research has been carried out, largely through the encouragement of the Amateur Yacht Research Society, an international body that has encouraged research into many aspects of sailing in general. So far, however, no sail or aerofoil-powered hydrofoil has been put into production. It is to be hoped the current research into military applications of this unique form of transport will lead to a breakthrough for the yachtsman, and the general acceptance of a novel new sailing "technique".

Aiming for speed

It is not just on hull configurations and design that research has been concentrated in recent years by enthusiasts. The whole principle of sail design and shape has come under close scrutiny and some interesting experiments in solid wings to provide the propulsion for a boat have been tried. Since the early days of flying it has been known that an aerofoil section provides forward as well as upward lift, and a yacht's sail has to be trimmed in such a way as to provide an aerofoil section. The next move was obviously to replace the canvas or Terylene sail-cloth which had to be trimmed to give the right shape with an aluminium "wing" manufactured to the right shape. This was tried reasonably successfully in Britain in the 1960s with a trimaran called *Planesail* which had three vertical wings. *Lady Helmsman*, a C Class catamaran reputed to be the fastest sailing boat in the world, had an aerofoil mast that effectively gave its sail a wing effect. The success of these experiments can be seen in *Miss Nylex*'s success in the Little America's Cup in 1974 in Australia.

For years yachtsmen have boasted of the speed attained by their boats, rather like fishermen with the size of fish that got away. Modern yacht speedometers, or logs, have introduced a certain amount of restraint, but the long-term answer has always been a measured distance and a team of timekeepers.

In 1972 the tobacco company, John Player, organized a week of speed trials at Weymouth in Britain, with a prize of £2,000 ($4,000) for the fastest boat. The entry list eventually included a standard planing monohull, a number of catamarans and trimarans and a few specially built hydrofoils and proas. The trial was illuminating in that all the boats were able to pick their own course and take as many runs as they liked during the week, but no one reached the speeds often claimed for their boats. The winner was *Crossbow* an 18.3 metres (60 foot) long proa designed by Rod Macalpine-Downie with an average speed of 26.3 knots over the 0.5 kilometre (550 yard) course. *Crossbow* was specifically designed for the competition and can in fact only sail on the starboard tack.

In 1973 the trials were held again and the top speed increased to 29.3 knots by a modified *Crossbow* which had had 1.5 metres (5 feet) removed from the stern to reduce "wetted surface". As *Crossbow* sailed well above what would be the normal speed for her waterline, length in this case was less important.

One of the more interesting designs in the competition in 1972 was *Clifton Flasher*. Unlike the other craft she did not use sails for her mode of propulsion, but instead had five low-speed aerofoil wings mounted vertically instead of horizontally. This is, in many ways, a logical extension of sailing theory in that a sail takes up an aerofoil section when trimmed. The difficulty with a set of fixed-section aerofoils is that they have a very narrow band of effective apparent wind in which they can operate, and thus lose efficiency rapidly when, say, trying to run off down wind. In the speed competition, however, *Clifton Flasher* was able to choose the optimum course, but further development of this interesting craft appeared necessary.

Such competitions have emphasized the distinctive speed advantages associated with the multihull concept. Development continues and multihull sailing seems destined for a· continued increase in popularity as more people discover the thrill of sailing at speeds previously only achieved in expensive motor boats.

CHAPTER 4

CRUISING

For those who do not want to compete in the racing circuits cruising provides an opportunity to get away from the hustle and bustle ashore; to wander where you wish with only the wind and sea to answer to and to be master of one's own destiny for a while. There is an incomparable sense of adventure in preparing your boat for sea, whether it be for a few days or for months, and whether you are going alone, with a friend or two, or with your family. For however long you plan to be away, you will shut yourself off from the world and become dependent upon your own resources, meanwhile getting plenty of exercise and breathing the cleanest air on the planet.

Just about any boat can be used for cruising—from the small dinghy that will take a couple on a day's picnic, through the 6–9 metres (20–30 foot) week-end sailing boat that will accommodate a family for a day or two, and the larger boats capable of taking a family for a fortnight, to finally the large luxury sailing boat with room for as many as four families.

Most racing boats do not make good cruising boats as they are designed to be manœuvred quickly and sailed hard with little consideration given to the comfort of the crew. The ideal cruiser should have good directional stability, a well-built seaworthy hull, plenty of room for people and stores and, above all, be capable of being sailed easily and safely by one or two people. As part of the fun in cruising is visiting areas you have not seen before, the ideal boat should be capable of lying alongside a quay or jetty at low tide without danger of tipping over, or should have twin bilge keels which are often found on boats kept in estuarial waters where deep-water mooring is not always available or convenient.

The shape of the hull is dependent upon the area you wish to cruise in. If you are going out into the open sea there is no point in having overhanging bows and sterns like a Dragon which are more suited to sheltered waters such as the Baltic. A fairly straight bow and deep forefoot give a more comfortable motion at sea, as there is nothing to slam back into the waves when the boat is pitching. Counter-sterns should be avoided because in a following sea the waves can get a lifting purchase at the stern and push the bows down. The safest stern is the canoe stern of the double-ended boat, such as a ship's lifeboat. Although in a following sea the stern will lift a bit, there is not a large reserve of buoyancy at this one end of the boat, and being pointed, it tends to cut into an overtaking wave so that it passes

A glass-fibre cruising boat designed for family use. The picture was taken in the Solent—a popular cruising water between the south coast of England and the Isle of Wight.

The saloon of a Westerly Tiger.

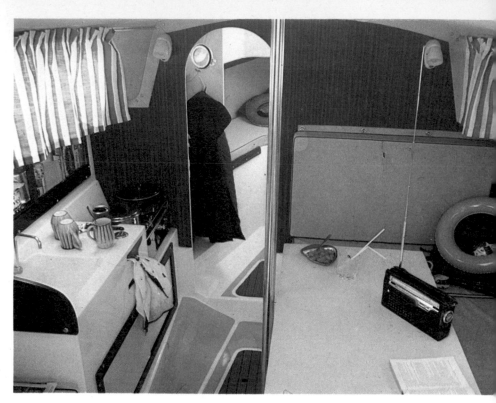

The Westerly Tiger is an ideal family cruiser.

harmlessly down either side of the boat. An added advantage is that the boat can lie either bow or stern to the sea in equal safety.

Cruising should not be undertaken without an engine in the boat, and most custom-built boats have one fitted. When you go away for a few days to a new area you should be able to motor in to the port. It may look smart to sail into harbour, but it is in fact exceedingly selfish and possibly dangerous. It is difficult to manœuvre as smartly under sail as under power and, therefore, more room is required. You are also asking others to take special care to see you have room, and there is not always a lot of space in a harbour or marina.

Many good cruising boat kits are available for home construction, and it is possible to buy a GRP hull and deck mouldings for most of the production boats and finish them off at home with a working knowledge of woodworking and plumbing. It is as well to have done some sailing first though, as you will appreciate better the reasons for extra strength round the mast and keel for instance, and why certain fittings go where they do.

Many people start off though by buying a second-hand boat. If you are going boat-hunting, check the brokerage pages of the yachting magazines first; not only will this give you an indication of the types of boat available and the asking prices, but you may find what you want straight off. When you do find the boat that suits you, always have a yacht surveyor in to look it over. The reason for this is that he will know what to look for and in most cases the survey report provides one or two bargaining points when you come to discuss the price. There is a belief that surveyors always find something wrong in

order to justify their fee, and I can remember once when the surveyor wrote that all the ventilators were rusty and should be re-galvanized—they were all made of Admiralty bronze! The main points to look out for when choosing your own boat are:

1. That you and your usual crew can handle the boat safely.
2. That, unless you are wealthy enough to have all your work done by boatyards, you and your crew can, and are willing to carry out all but major maintenance work. Remember a boat is far more complicated than a car and requires far more attention.
3. That the boat has sufficient space for people and stores.
4. That you have a safe place to moor the boat.
5. That the boat is seaworthy.

Before going on a cruise the boat should be checked over thoroughly to ensure that all the rigging and equipment are in good order. Start

Boats under construction in the Camper Nicholson yard at Gosport in Hampshire.

off with the hull and check that all the seacocks are greased and the bilge-pumps work. If the boat is taking more water than you expected, discover why and fix it. The sea is not the place for complicated repairs and your crew will not appreciate pumping themselves into port. Check over the masts and rigging and if the rigging is old or looks doubtful, renew it. Remember that when you are under sail, the rigging will be taking all the strain of the weight of the wind in the sails. If one piece of rigging breaks, the mast will most likely collapse and you will be left with the engine or setting up a jury rig in order to find a port. A jury rig is any make-do system and in this case refers to hoisting sail once the mainmast has broken. There may be, for instance, a reasonable length of mast left which can be lashed up and a sail set on it, or the main boom might suffice. Either of these would be a jury mast.

You should certainly check the sails and running rigging before setting out. (Running rigging is a rope or wire in the rigging that moves, such as a halyard, sheet, etc., as opposed to standing rigging which is fixed—like a stay or shroud.) The best method is to take each sail out of its sail bag in turn, bend it on, and hoist it. In this way you check the sheet halyards, winches and blocks as well as the sail itself. If there is any fray anywhere get the sail sewn up immediately. Remember that the expression 'a stitch in time saves nine' originated with sailmakers, and if you do not follow this old adage you are going to do a lot of sewing.

Check the engine, and have it serviced before you go. The electrical system suffers from damp. Also on many marine engines the water-cooling pump is driven by a fan belt and if it breaks the engine will over-heat and eventually seize up. Always carry a spare. Top up your fuel-tank before you leave, it may not be convenient always to obtain fuel at ports where you call.

Water-tanks always require atten-

The Westerley Medway—a 12 metre glass-fibre family cruiser.

tion and are well worth the effort whatever they are made of. It is well worth draining the tank and refilling it with fresh water before setting off. If the tank has got a bit stagnant empty it out and then put in fresh water with a few tablets of potassium permanganate. Leave this for a few days and then pump out again. Finally fill and empty the tank again before filling up for the voyage. There is nothing worse than evil-tasting water when at sea, at best it means foul-tasting coffee, at worst stomach upsets. It is possible to gather rainwater at sea in an emergency. The best method is to use the mainsail as a rain-catcher and to top up the main boom so that the water will run down it to the gooseneck. This means you have only one collection point, and it is comparatively easy to hold a bucket under the gooseneck to catch the water. Do not start collecting the water as soon as the rain begins to fall, wait a minute or so until the sail and boom have been "freshed off". Pure rainwater has a complete-

ly different taste to ordinary fresh water, try cups of coffee from both to sample the difference.

Safety

Never put to sea without checking the boat's safety equipment. To start with, check that there are enough lifejackets and safety-harnesses on board for each member of the crew. Next check the liferaft or dinghy, and if you only carry a dinghy, make sure it has no leaks. If it is an inflatable, ensure you have the repair kit and pump aboard. The boat should carry at least one lifebuoy, placed where it can be quickly released and thrown to someone in the water. Nowadays a lot of boats carry special buoys attached to the lifebuoy which carry a flag and flashing light on a stick above the water so that it can be seen more readily.

Every boat must carry a fog-horn, either the compressed-air type, a freon-powered horn, or one you can blow with your mouth. I favour

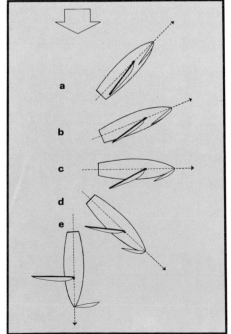

Far left: The essential points of sailing. From top to bottom the positions are close-hauled, close reach, reach, broad reach and run. Knowledge of these terms is essential before setting out on a cruise.

Left: a Finrose 37 photographed beating in a fresh breeze.

the latter two as they won't run out on a long voyage or if you run into a few days' fog.

Distress rockets and flares and smoke floats are essential. If you get into distress you will want to give as much time to the lifesaving organizations as possible. The longer you leave it, the harder their task and the less your chance of survival. In recent years there have been a number of cases where people in distress have sent off flares when they have seen a ship and there has been no response. Remember that a ship at sea does not expect to see a distress flare, and the crews of modern ships are not about the decks as they used to be. Before sending off a rocket in these circumstances, try to work out the path the ship is going to take, and fire the rocket so that it will explode in front of the ship when it is as

close to you as it is going to be. This gives you the greatest chance of being seen as the wheelhouse, which is probably manned, faces forward.

Do not neglect your medical kit or a good first aid book. Most countries publish official ships' medical guides, and many Americans consider that the Red Cross First Aid Handbook is invaluable.

No small boat can go far wrong if it carries the equipment specified for a ship's lifeboat as far as general safety gear is concerned, and most Governments publish these requirements. This makes very interesting reading. The U.S. Government has, in fact, specified certain items of equipment that must, by law, be carried on all pleasure boats. A word of warning concerning the use of sea anchors though. These cone-shaped canvas bags are designed to hold the boat's head up into the sea on the end of a stout line. They perform this task very effectively. In order to recover the sea anchor, however, a tripping line is attached to the narrow end of the cone so that the brake can be let go. Unless particular care is taken, the tripping line has a nasty habit of getting itself entangled with the anchor. An alternative is to use a hawser paid out over the bow, or if the boat is a double ender then it can be paid out over the stern. If both ends of the hawser are made fast on board so that a loop is in the water, quite a braking force can be exerted and this force can be increased or decreased by lengthening or shortening the loop.

Navigation and navigation aids

Navigation is as important to the safety of a boat and crew as life-

Opposite above: two crew with the safety equipment that all boats should carry.

Opposite below: a day's sailing over, the crew of this old gaffer prepare to take in the foresails.

High speed rescue launches such as this one are widely used nowadays.

jackets and distress flares, but it is frequently taken for granted. The ability to be able to pinpoint your position both in sight and out of sight of land, in fog or clear visibility is essential and does wonders for the crew's morale!

Do not forget your charts and sailing instructions. Apart from their primary use of guiding you away from danger, there is much other useful and interesting information on a chart. Make sure that your

Navigation instruments being used to plot a course on a chart.

charts are up to date. In Britain, the Admiralty publishes weekly *Notices to Mariners* which are issued free by Shipping Offices and Chart Depots in Britain, and by Consuls abroad. These give the correction to the British Charts, but of course the corrections would apply to any charts. These corrections are numbered, and as a chart is corrected the number is written on the bottom right-hand margin of the chart. In this way you can quickly tell whether all the corrections are made neatly and accurately. U.S. Coastguards publish local Notices to Mariners and these are available free from district headquarters. Charts should

always be kept clean and carefully folded away when not in use. Nothing harder than a 2B pencil should ever be used on a chart, as this can be easily erased leaving the chart clean for the next time it may be required.

Charts are expensive and there is no need to buy every chart covering the area you are going to sail. Study the Chart Atlas and buy the large-scale chart that shows your start-point and destination. This will be your routing chart. Then buy only those others that are necessary; for instance, the approaches to land, the ports themselves, and also the charts to one or two "funk holes" along the route in case the weather turns against you. When I sailed round the world I took only thirteen charts, and I could have usefully taken only four more covering the coasts of Australia and New Zealand.

The one piece of information that may be missing from a chart is the light characteristic and position of buoys although they are available on National Survey Charts. Most countries publish a series of light lists which cover every navigation light in the world, and the book that deals with the area you are going to cruise is an essential occupant of your bookshelf. You will see on the chart that each light has a limit of visibility written next to it. These distances were calculated for a height of 4.5 metres (15 feet), the height of the average man's eye when standing on the poop deck of a sailing ship. If you are standing on the deck of a yacht, your height of eye is your height plus the yacht's freeboard. This is probably less than the calculated height, so you will have to sail closer to the light than the distance given on the chart before you will see it.

When you are navigating along the coast you will be able to check your position regularly by means of bearings taken off prominent objects such as headlands, lighthouses and buildings. You should cross-check these with a sounding either with an echo-sounder or a lead line. Lead lines are not often seen these days, but they are a very reliable method of discovering the depth of water beneath your boat. In the old days, when there was no other method, the seamen used to "arm" the lead by putting tallow or beeswax in a small hole in the bottom of the lead weight. When this hit the bottom, small particles would stick to the tallow and the seaman would know whether the sea's bottom was sand, gravel, clay or whatever. He could check this with his chart which showed the nature of the bottom by means of the small abbreviations which you can still see on a modern chart. Do not forget when taking a sounding close to land that the chart shows the depth of water at Mean Low Water Springs (in U.S. Mean Lower Low Water) whereas your sounding will show the depth the time you are in a particular spot. Deduct the height of the tide from your sounding before looking at the chart.

A useful modern aid to navigation is the Radio Direction Finder. Dotted round the coasts of the world are transmitters that issue a radio signal at pre-given times which starts off with an identification signal in the morse code, and then gives a steady note. With a radio receiver and a directional aerial, it is possible to pick up these stations and then, by revolving the aerial in the horizontal plane, alter the note of the signal. When the lowest note is found take the bearing and this bearing *or* its reciprocal is the bearing of you from the radio beacon. You can usually tell which of the two bearings is the right one,

but if in doubt draw both on the chart, and take a bearing of another beacon and draw that on the chart as well. Your approximate position is where the two bearings cross. Radio bearings are meant to be accurate to within a couple of degrees, but it takes practice and ideal conditions to achieve this. Remember radio bearings are inaccurate during twilight because of atmospheric interference, so do not take bearings then.

A familiar sight to sailors the world over —Plymouth pictured at dawn on a summer's day.

Signalling

In the old days flags were used for signalling, and an *international flag code* was developed so that ships of different nations and languages could communicate easily. This code still exists, and can be used by any yacht for signalling another yacht or shore signal station. Each of the alphabetical flags has an individual meaning which is essential knowledge for a seaman and should be learned off by heart.

The *morse code* is another method of communicating at sea—signals being transmitted by means of a light. Special signalling lamps can be bought, but a torch with a press-button on/off switch will do.

Many yachts now fit radio telephone so that they can put a call through to the shore while far out at sea. The cheapest form of radio telephone uses only Very High Frequency channels and is known as *VHF*. These sets have a limited range of only about 48 kilometres (30 miles). For longer ranges Medium Frequencies are used, but basically the range of a radio depends very much on the transmitter's power output and the efficiency of the aerial. It is possible for instance to hold a conversation over 8,000 kilometres (5,000 miles) on a frequency of 16 megahertz with a radio using the yacht's 12 or 24 volt batteries, but a radio set like this will cost five times as much as a VHF.

Radio stations are set up all over the world for the use of merchant ships and fishing vessels and it is these stations you can call to if you want to send a message. The only difference between using a radio telephone and the telephone in your home is that to avoid distortion only one person can speak at a time on the radio telephone. Over long distances it is often difficult to hear a person properly and so an international phonetic alphabet has been developed so that words can be spelled out if necessary. Instead

Below: radio telephones are widely used to send and receive messages at sea.

Below right: Robin Knox-Johnston uses his sextant to take a sight so that he can accurately plot his position and plan the next leg of his voyage.

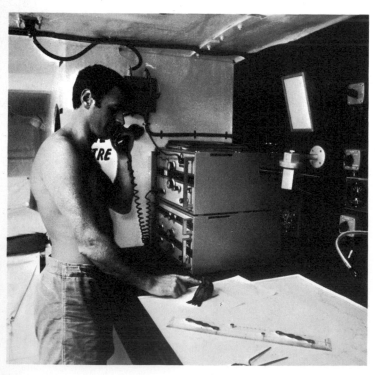

of spelling out A, B, C, etc. you would use: Alpha, Bravo, Charlie, Delta, Echo, Foxtrot, Golf, Hotel, India, Juliet, Kilo, Lima, Mike, November, Oscar, Papa, Quebec, Romeo, Sierra, Tango, Uniform, Victor, Whiskey, X-ray, Yankee, Zulu. These words are difficult to confuse with each other, and the sounds are distinguishable when other words are not.

Sextants

Astro-navigation, or the use of a sextant and altitudes of the Sun, Moon, planets or stars is a separate subject in itself. But a sextant has other uses, for instance the height of the light in a lighthouse is always given on charts, and by measuring the angle subtended by the light and the base of the lighthouse you can calculate your distance from it. These are called *vertical sextant angles*. Another method of fixing your position when in sight of land is by means of *horizontal sextant angles*. In this you measure the angle subtended horizontally to you between three objects ashore that are clearly marked on the chart. By means of some fairly simple geometry a very accurate position can be found. Obviously if you have an accurate hand-bearing compass you could obtain the answer much more quickly with that, but the sextant method is much more accurate.

The use of a sextant in a small boat requires a fair amount of practice especially if the boat is heaving about. As both hands are needed I usually sit on the coach roof, or hook an arm round a shroud to steady myself. If the sextant gets salt spray on it, wash it off immediately with distilled or fresh water or it will begin to corrode. A sextant is more than a device for measuring angles, it is a highly sophisticated scientific instrument and deserves respect.

Provisions

The sort of food you decide to take is a matter of personal preference and availability. Before buying anything, however, settle down and work out how many meals you are going to have to cook for the number of crew on board and the expected number of days you expect to be away. I always find it advisable to make out a menu list for a voyage of up to a week's duration; there is nothing worse than repetitive feeding. For instance, if you have a crew of seven people and you expect a voyage to take a week, the calculation is fairly simple. First allow a safety margin of about 25 per cent. Remember, sailing boats have destinations and not estimated times of arrival, and it is difficult accurately to predict when you will reach your destination. So in this case I would take enough food for nine days. This means you have got to have sufficient food on board for 63 breakfasts, 63 lunches and 63 dinners. Work out menus for nine breakfasts, lunches and dinners and avoid repeating anything if you can. Now all you have to do is write down the food required for each meal in turn and you have your shopping list. Where possible use fresh food, meat for instance can be kept for a fortnight in a freeze-box packed with dry ice. Usually, however, apart from things like eggs and potatoes, the bulk of the food will have to be in tins or packets. Store the tins in a dry place if possible, and if your voyage is only expected to last a week or so they will probably be all right. On a longer voyage though it is advisable to protect tins as few boats are completely dry and sooner or later the labels start to come off and the tin will rust. The best protection is a coat of varnish but before doing this make up a code and paint it on the tin. There is nothing worse than opening a tin of what you think is steak for a stew only to discover that in fact you have got fruit! Once your tins are coded, tear off the labels and then apply a coat of varnish. Reasonably stowed the tins will last a year or more.

Tins usually show if their contents have gone off, as the ends get blown out. If in doubt, immerse the tin in heated sea-water and if bubbles start to come from the tin, throw it away immediately. Meat and fish are evil smelling when they go off, and vegetables ferment, neither will do anyone any good, and will most likely lead to food poisoning. A small boat is not the place for sickness.

It is, of course, quite possible to supplement your food by fishing. Around coasts and over continental shelves it is well worth having a trolling line out with a spinner on the end. A freshly caught herring or mackerel frying in a pan of butter has a smell one can never forget. Out at sea, the colour of the water is greenish. This denotes the presence of algae which is at the bottom end of the food chain and so fish are likely to be present. If the water is blue it is generally empty, but you may find the odd small school of dorado or bonito. Both are excellent eating. The dorado is also interesting as it changes from its green, blue and silver colour to blue and silver as it dies. These fish have probably never seen a human before and will come in close to you if you are swimming in the water so you can catch them with a spear-gun. Flying fish are very tasty, and when you get down towards the tropics they

will often land on board during the night, providing you with an excellent fresh breakfast.

In recent years ocean voyages by small boats have become an almost everyday event, and we are always reading of a family that has just completed a voyage of many thousands of miles in safety. It is worth remembering though that these voyages are not completed by luck, but by hard work and attention to detail when planning the trip.

A very adventurous family cruise was the circumnavigation of the world by New Zealander David Lewis and his family in the catamaran *Rehu Moana* between 1964 and 1967. *Rehu Moana* completed the 1964 single-handed race, and Mrs Lewis and the two small children, one only six months old, joined David Lewis in America. They then set off for Cape Horn calling at the Cape Verde Islands and ports in Brazil on the way. After a harrowing passage through the Magellan Strait, they headed for Valparaiso and then set course for New Zealand. On the way Dr Lewis sailed the 2,560 kilometres (1,600 miles) from Tahiti to New Zealand

A Finrose 37 bermudan-rigged sloop showing her paces off the Rock of Gibraltar. She can sleep up to six people in a great deal of comfort and is fitted with an auxiliary diesel engine.

entirely without navigation instruments, relying upon the Polynesian methods of watching the birds and sailing by the stars. From New Zealand the family sailed across the Indian Ocean to Durban and then back to England via the Cape of Good Hope.

David Lewis is a doctor, and an expert on Polynesian navigation, and he had other voyages under his belt which gave him invaluable experience before he set off with his very young family. His preparations, however, had to be doubly thorough because of the extra special stores required aboard his floating nursery. At the end of the voyage, the two little girls were totally adjusted to their shipboard life, and found life ashore very strange in comparison.

Although this voyage is not typical of the average family sailing cruise, it shows that even long voyages are perfectly safe in a small boat with a very young family and I quote it as an encouragement to those who feel that these problems are insurmountable.

Long ocean voyages, whether single-handed or with a crew, are the dream for most sailors, but only a very small proportion achieve them. For those who can find the time, the oceans are still a vast area, unpredictable and unexplored, where man can come face to face with the elements with only his skill and determination to see him through to his destination. Going to sea is not opting out, it is opting in to a challenge and responsibility that cannot be switched off like the radio until you are safely moored.

For those prepared to make the effort whether as skipper or crew, the challenge is always there and the rewards are great but personal.

There is nothing quite like sailing into a strange foreign port after a few days at sea, piloting carefully towards the yacht basin or mooring, and finally tying up, hoping that you have not pinched someone else's private mooring. You look around wondering to whom you should report and suddenly a small boat comes out to you, takes everyone aboard and runs you into the local yacht club for a drink and a bath. You have brought your craft safely into port, and even Columbus could hardly have felt better when he returned to Spain.

CHAPTER 5

OCEAN RACING

Modern ocean racing owes as much to the rating systems within which craft are classified as it does to the men who pioneered small ocean-going yachts. Boats will race each other regardless of differences in size, displacement and rig, but usually the larger boat will win. Rating committees have taken all the varying factors, and calculated ratings which, when applied to the actual finishing times in a race, will give handicap times. Thus, although large boats will usually cross the line first (line honours), small boats can be declared the actual winners on corrected time. The moment the owner of a small boat thinks he has a chance of beating a larger boat, for a handicap prize, he feels encouraged to enter a race, and so competition improves. Since 1969 the International Offshore Rule, known as the *IOR* has been accepted on a world-wide basis. This allows a boat built and rated in Argentina to cross to Europe knowing in advance how she compares with the European boats and to enter the local races on equal terms.

This is the essence of modern ocean racing and one of the reasons why the sport has grown so dramatically over the last decade. It is possible for a production-line boat to enter the same race as enormously expensive specially built boats of many times her size and to win. Although in serious distance racing the expensive custom-built yachts tend to do better than production boats.

Ocean racing as an organized sport really started in the United States at the beginning of the 20th century. There had been races across oceans before, but normally these had been spontaneous competitions between two or three owners. One of the earliest recorded was held in 1866 when three American schooners, *Henrietta*, *Vesta* and *Fleetwing* raced across the Atlantic. In 1905 Kaiser Wilhelm II of Germany offered a Gold Cup as the prize for a transatlantic race, but this was a one-off event and not a regularly organized race.

The Bermuda and Fastnet Races

The first Bermuda Race, in 1906 was little different. T. F. Day, the editor of the magazine *Rudder* and a vigorous exponent of the seaworthiness of small boats, organized the race from New York to Bermuda, a distance of 960 kilometres (600 miles) in order to prove that small boats could race that far in safety. The race was, however, such a success that it was repeated in 1923, and when the Cruising Club of America was formed, the organization of the race was passed on to the new club and its future assured.

The American yacht Carina beating to windward during the second inshore race for the Admiral's Cup in 1971. The United States were second in the race.

The crew of *Rubin* (Germany) adjusting sheets, during one of the 1975 Admiral's Cup races.

Opposite above: Admiral's Cup contenders race downwind showing a brilliant display of spinnakers.

Opposite below: Yankee Girl, *pride of the American Admiral's Cup team in 1971, leads the field during the Second Inshore race.*

Day's arguments received even greater support in 1906 from another race organized on the West Coast of America. The Transpac Race from Los Angeles to Honolulu, is over 3,680 kilometres (2,300 miles) long, and until 1971 was the longest ocean race in the calendar.

It was nearly twenty years before anyone else started a race that came near to equalling these two American classics. This came about when an Englishman took part in the 1924 Bermuda Race. He was so impressed that in 1925 he organized a race of similar length on the east side of the Atlantic, the Fastnet Race.

The first Fastnet Race was won by a converted Havre pilot cutter, the *Jolie Brise*, owned by George Martin. The British were still using converted work boats for ocean cruising and the first Fastnet Race was very much a cruisers' race. The enthusiasm of the competitors after the race was such that they formed a new club to organize the event again and to encourage similar races. This was the Ocean Racing Club, and Martin was the first Commodore. In 1931 the club became the Royal Ocean Racing Club. The Fastnet Race caught on very quickly. Unlike the Bermuda Race where the winds are predictable and a reaching course normal, or the Transpac Race where conditions are likely to repeat themselves, the Fastnet Race weather can never be predicted and the navigator is kept constantly busy with the tides that swirl round the south-western tip of Great Britain.

Perhaps this was its attraction, for in 1931 the Americans came over to try their hand at something different and ran away with the race. The boat that won looked very like the boats to be found competing round the buoys at Cowes at the time rather than the chunky work boats sailed by the British. The Americans were still showing the way as far as ocean racing was concerned, and *Dorade*, designed by a new young designer, Olin Stephens, showed how wide the gap was. *Dorade* won again in 1933, and in 1935 a new Stephens design *Stormy Weather* was the winner. It was not until 1939 that the British attempted to catch up with *Bloodhound* designed by Charles E. Nicholson. After World War II she was sold to the British Royal Family, but she could not be tested against the American proven strength as the war clouds in Europe discouraged any Americans from coming over that year.

The Fastnet and Bermuda Races are held in alternate years, the Fastnet in odd years and the Bermuda in the even, so that they do not clash. It was not until 1945 that another "classic", the Sydney–Hobart Race, was started by the Royal Yacht Club of Tasmania. The Sydney–Hobart now forms the most important race in an international series known as the Southern Cross Series, with a 160 kilometre (100 mile) race from Sydney to Flinders Island and back and two inshore 48 kilometre (30 mile) races.

The appeal of ocean racing

Uffa Fox, the British yachtsman, once described ocean racing as being similar to standing beneath a cold shower tearing up £5 notes as fast as one can. The Duke of Edinburgh added that this applied to the skippers, but the crew's job was more akin to sitting inside a washing machine that has been turned on. Most people who go ocean racing will agree that there is an element of truth in both these comments, but they still go sailing. It is difficult to see why people should wish to spend their leisure time threshing around in a small wet boat, getting plenty of bruises but little sleep and returning at the end with nothing to show for it all but aching muscles and possibly a silver cup that can be kept for a year. What is the magic about ocean racing that sees the numbers taking it up increase year by year all over the world?

One answer must be that while it is a physical sport, mental stamina is also very important. It is a highly competitive and skilful sport, in which experience is more important than youthful vigour. It is possible to continue to go ocean racing successfully long after most other sports have had to be given up.

To watch the start of a race is misleading. The boats tack in a seemingly aimless manner until just before the start gun, when they all suddenly turn towards the start line as if controlled by one invisible thread. On board at this moment there is an air of tense expectancy. The skipper is heading for the start line as the navigator counts down to

the gun, aiming to be just short of the line as the gun goes. The first leg of the race will already be known and the navigator will have worked out the tides and calculated the most favourable course to take. The crew will be watching intently, in case, in the rush for the line the boat is caught by another boat which the racing rules dictate must be given the right of way. If this happens the skipper will have split seconds to decide on his course of action, change course and look for another gap. As the boat comes round, the foredeck hands will be hauling the clew of the sail round the mast and in the cockpit there will be a frantic burst of winch-winding to haul the sheets in as quickly as possible to get the boat moving again on the new course. If the skipper miscalculates, the boat will foul another boat and be disqualified, or be involved in an expensive collision which could mean withdrawing from the race.

When the race is started down wind, spinnakers—large light nylon sails usually highly coloured—will be set just before the start and all the boats will head off in the same direction. When the start is into the wind the boats will have to tack their way to the first mark of the course. This is far more wearying for the crew as the constant winch work is tiring; it also requires full alertness from the helmsman as the boat on the port tack gives way to one on the starboard tack, and the helmsman must constantly watch that he is going to clear a crossing boat.

The real action in a racing yacht comes when the boats change sail or round a mark where they have just finished a run or are about to start one. If the boats are beating towards the mark and a run is to follow, the spinnaker will have to

be hoisted as the mark is rounded. The foredeck hands will rig the spinnaker pole, a light aluminium pole almost exactly the same length as the distance between the mast and the bow, and if it is clear this will be braced into position. The light nylon spinnaker is then taken forward in its bag and the top end, known as the *head*, clipped on to a halyard which will be used to hoist the sail. The other two ends are clipped on to their sheets, ropes

Racing downwind with the spinnakers set.

coming up on either side of the boat, one through the pole to give stability. As the yacht comes round the mark, the order is given to hoist and the cockpit crew haul the top of the sail up to the masthead by the halyard. At the same time they have to take in the slack on the sheets. The foredeck crew have the job of seeing that the sail is hoisted freely and opens up immediately. In a 48 kilometre (30 mile race) one second can make the difference between first and second place and there is no time to be lost. Once the spinnaker is hoisted and is pulling, the headsail, or jib will usually be taken down and stowed on deck ready to be rehoisted. The yacht has started a run with the wind coming from astern and unless the wind is particularly strong she will be on an even keel. The crew can remove their oilskins and dry out for a while or at least until the next sail change or mark of the course.

Setting spinnakers having just rounded the windward mark.

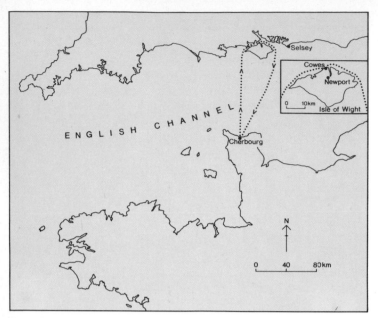

THE CROSS CHANNEL RACE

In a week-end race this sequence can be repeated many times, and each time the whole crew will have to come out on deck as all hands are needed if a manœuvre is to be carried out quickly and efficiently. Nowadays there will always be other boats in sight and no crew wants to look sloppy.

Once the race is over, win or lose, the boat must be tidied up, all the sails used in the race, perhaps as many as twenty, dried out and folded away for the next time. The crew will be tired but already beginning to look forward to the next race.

The Admiral's Cup

The best-known international ocean-racing competition is the Admiral's Cup, a series of four races sailed every other year and organized by the Royal Ocean Racing Club. The cup, originally presented in 1957 by Sir Myles Wyatt, then Admiral of the RORC, is for international teams of three boats from each country and is awarded to the team gaining the most points in the series of races. Unlike most other international competitions, the Admiral's Cup is always held in British waters and always consists of four specified races: the Channel Race— 362 kilometres (230 miles); the Britannia Cup—48 kilometres (30 miles); the New York Yacht Club Cup—48 kilometres (30 miles); and the Fastnet—968 kilometres (605 miles). The races are timed to coincide with Cowes Week with the Channel Race at the beginning, the two short races during the week and the Fastnet Race starting on the final Saturday. The cup is awarded to the team gaining the most points in the four races. The boat's position on handicap in the race decides the

points earned, so that if there are 48 boats in the race the first boat receives 48 points and the last 1 point. The Channel Race counts as double points and the Fastnet Race as treble. Although the first three races provide an indication of a team's strength, it is almost impossible for the cup to have been conclusively won before the Fastnet Race, and this maintains the suspense right to the end of the series.

Since the first Admiral's Cup Series in 1957, when five nations competed, the regatta has grown to the extent that eighteen nations competed in 1973 and in many countries the teams were chosen after a series of hard-fought elimination races.

In 1957 and 1959 Britain successfully defended the cup against America, Sweden, Holland and France. In 1961, however, a strong American team including two new boats *Cyane* and *Windrose* took the cup to the States. The British reply in 1963 came from six new boats especially launched for the challenge, and the final team of *Clarion of Wight, Outlaw* and *Noryema III* recovered the cup. The next series produced the first serious Australian challenge among the eight national teams from Ireland, Germany, Sweden, Holland, America and France. The British team consisted of three more new boats *Firebrand, Quiver IV* and *Noryema IV*. The Australian team was *Caprice of Huon, Freya* and *Camille of Seaforth*. After the Channel Race, Britain led by four points and increased the lead in the Britannia Cup, although *Caprice* won both races. The strength and determination behind the Australian challenge is best illustrated by *Camille* in this second race. When she finished she was disqualified for

going round a buoy the wrong way. Realizing that there was no time limit for the race *Camille* put out again and resailed the last leg of the race, recovering six points for Australia. *Caprice* won the New York Yacht Club Cup in a race where Britain fared badly, but the Fastnet Race was a British triumph and the cup remained in England.

The Australians came back in strength for the 1967 series and won by a margin of 104 points with Britain second and the United States and France close behind. The 1967 series was enlivened by individual successes for America in the inshore races when Dick Carter's *Rabbit II* won both the Britannia and New

York Cups although he retired later from the Britannia, and by Eric Tabarly of France with *Pen Duick III* who won the Channel Race and the Fastnet.

The year 1969 saw a strong American challenge with *Red Rooster, Carina* and *Palawan*. The two latter boats were large and did

Opposite above: the course of the cross-Channel Admiral's Cup Race.

Opposite below: stowing the genoa after a spinnaker hoist.

Eric Tabarly, skipper of Pen Duick VI, making last-minute adjustments before setting out on the Whitbread Round the World Race in 1973.

so well in the Fastnet that the United States moved from third place before the race to take the cup in the end. The Australians came second with Britain third and Italy fourth.

Fourteen nations entered in 1971 and Britain had no fewer than 27 contestants from which to choose a team. Eventually *Morning Cloud*, owned and sailed by the British Prime Minister, Edward Heath, *Prospect of Whitby* and *Cervantes* were chosen. After some heavy nail-biting, particularly after *Cervantes* was disqualified in the second race, Britain won the cup with America second, Australia third and Argentina fourth.

The continuing expansion of interest in the race is shown by the sixteen national entries that entered in the 1973 competition and the fact that Britain sailed selection races with no fewer than 32 participants. The first races were run in strong wind conditions that were expected to suit the Australian trio *Apollo*, *Ginko* and *Ragamuffin*. But the German boat *Saudade* sailed by

Berend Beilkin came through best with a fourth in the Channel Race and wins in both the shorter inshore races. Britain lay second to the Germans before the Fastnet Race and the Australians third. Once again the series hinged on the Fastnet Race which provided a complete contrast to the other races as the wind fell very light. It seemed at one point, with the first fourteen boats home, that Britain would retain the cup as two of the British team *Quailo* and *Frigate* were home and well placed. All three German boats were in, but if the third British boat, *Morning Cloud* could get in quickly, the handicap position was such that Britain would win. *Morning Cloud* unfortunately became becalmed some 16 kilometres (10 miles) from the finish and as the hours slipped by the German position strengthened. The final result was a win for Germany, with Australia second. Britain regained the cup in 1975 with *Noryema*, *Yeoman XX* and *Battlecry*.

The Admiral's Cup has now become one of the world's premier offshore racing series and so dominates the offshore scene that many owners now use the latest in design and equipment to build boats in a two-year cycle for team selection.

Newly established ocean races

The competitive urge to race yachts has attracted increasing interest in recent years, so much so that most of the established races have reached entry numbers where the race committees, who arrange the starts, supervise the finishes and decide upon any dispute between the competitors, have to be organized on almost military lines. The increase in numbers of competitors has also presented a navigation problem as most of the races take place in waters frequented by commercial shipping and a very real danger of collision exists when 200–300 yachts are set off on a race across crowded shipping lanes.

One result of this crowding has been the introduction of new races of longer duration in places farther from the major sea routes. One

Ragamuffin.

of these races is the Middle Sea Race organized by the Royal Malta Yacht Club from Valetta in Malta, round Lampedusa and Sicily and back to Malta. This race was first sailed in 1967 and attracted British, French and Italian yachts as well as a strong contingent from Malta itself. This course is 971 kilometres (607 miles) or the equivalent of the Bermuda or Fastnet Race. By 1973 the number of competitors had increased substantially and in only five years the race has become a well-established fixture.

Continuing the trend, an even longer race for fully crewed ocean racers was organized in 1971 by the South African Cruising Association in conjunction with the Yate Club de Rio, for a race over 5,600 kilometres (3,500 miles) between Cape Town and Rio de Janiero. Some 59 boats started from Cape Town and all but one, which claimed to have hit a whale and sunk as a result, completed the race.

As an added attraction the yachts arrived in Rio in time for the famous Mardi Gras Festival, a more hazardous event than the race itself. The Cape–Rio Race was sailed again in 1973 with a slightly smaller entry and was won by Dutch/South African Kees Bruynzeel in *Stormy* which provided a fitting end to an ocean-racing career spanning four decades. This race has quickly established itself in the ocean-racing calendar despite the distance from the well-established yacht-racing centres.

In 1973 an even more elaborate race was organized by the Royal Naval Sailing Association for a fully crewed Class 1 IOR race round the world, starting from Portsmouth in England with a first

Saudade (Germany) on a downhill run in the 1973 Admiral's Cup First Inshore race.

leg of 11,200 kilometres (7,000 miles) to Cape Town. After a short break the yachts continued to Sydney in Australia then on to Rio de Janiero in Brazil, with the final leg being sailed as a pursuit race and all the yachts being set off in reverse order of their handicap ratings so that, in theory, they would all arrive back at Portsmouth together early in April 1974.

Each of the four legs of this race was at least ten times as long as a Bermuda, Middle Sea or Fastnet Race and presented logistical problems not particularly common in ocean racing. Not surprisingly, the first leg was won by the Royal Navy entry *Adventure* with a crew of reasonably experienced racing men. In fact Leslie Williams, an experienced offshore racing helmsman, crossed the line first in *Burton Cutter*. The Frenchman Eric

Pinta (Germany). After the First Inshore race in 1975, Germany was leading in the Admiral's Cup competition, but after the Second Inshore and Fastnet Races Britain regained the Cup.

The 1973 Cup races saw many closely fought duels such as this one between Morning Cloud *(UK)* and Salty Goose *(US).*

Tabarly was in the lead on this leg when he broke his mainmast, an accident which cost him his chance of winning the race over all. Ocean racing is not just pushing a boat as hard as the boat will go, it is a balance between a competitive urge to win and seamanship, where knowing the limit of your boat and her crew and equipment is all important.

The second stage to Sydney provided considerable drama. First *Burton Cutter* began to break up and withdrew. Then a man was lost overboard from the French entry. The leg was won by the Mexican boat *Sayula II* which built up an indisputable lead, and went on to win the race with *Adventure* second.

Even as the RNSA race was taking place, a second, fully crewed Round the World Race was being planned which started from London in August 1975 with four entrants from Italy, France, Holland and Britain. This race had only one stop in Sydney, Australia.

The next logical step is another non-stop round the world competition, but first, in 1977, there is to be another race which will include multihulls as well.

A sport for the rich?

While the aristocrats of the ocean-racing scene, the Class I boats costing more than most people earn in a lifetime, may get most of the attention, the smaller offshore racers are rapidly coming into their own with the One Ton, Half Ton and more recently the Quarter Ton classes. The Quarter Ton Class has provided a much-needed bridge between the dinghy men and the offshore racing fraternity, where dinghy techniques are carried through to almost extreme lengths in order to get the fastest boat of the lowest possible rating.

Adventure — the winner of the Portsmouth–Cape Town leg of the 1973 Whitbread Round the World Race.

Class I boats run from 11 metres (33 feet) of rating up to 24 metres (70 feet). Bearing in mind that these are rating limits and not actual dimensions, this means that an average Class I boat is between 15 and 29 metres (44 and 80 feet) in length. Class divisions do not apply in the United States where races are divided into Divisions and a boat can race in different divisions.

The other classes are divided up by rating. Thus Class II includes boats from 9 to 10 metres (29 to 33 feet) rating; Class III of 8–9 metres (25.5–29 feet); Class IV 7–8 metres (23–25.5 feet) and Class V 6–7 metres (21–23 feet). The reason for these class divisions is to enable the organizers to split the starts of races and avoid having too many boats all rushing for the line at once. It also means that if the weather is more suitable for the larger boats, the smaller boats can still race for their own class victory.

A recent development, although

in many respects it is a throwback to the pre-war "metre" and "letter" classes, is the level-rating races. In this type of racing a particular IOR rating figure is chosen and all boats of that rating race together. Boats will be built for a particular rating and all the signs point to a rapid expansion of this development, as the complexities of calculating position after a race under the usual IOR conditions, mean that often the result of a race is not known until the last boat has arrived. In Level Rating Racing, the first boat over the line is the winner.

The bigger boats have now reached the stage where costs prohibit too much experimentation. The small Quarter Ton boats on the other hand can be built reasonably inexpensively and this has resulted in some interesting and novel ideas from a new breed of designers. Generally, yachts have always been a compromise between a heavy boat that will smash through the waves into the wind, and a light boat that will be more easily driven down wind. The recent trend has been towards finding a light boat that can be given sufficient power through having a large sail area to go well to windward. In order to keep the boat as near upright as possible stability has to be increased by means other than a heavy keel and the result has been a trend towards almost absurdly wide boats.

The modern ocean racer is a highly expensive and complex racing machine. The rough price of a 13 metre (40 foot) boat in 1973 was £80,000 ($150,000).

The hull could be constructed of wood, steel, aluminium or glass fibre to a design which, after tank testing, could easily amount to £6,000 ($13,000). Masts and spars are usually of aluminium and the rigging of stainless steel. Rod rigging is now more common than wire, as it has less stretch. Bottle screws (turnbuckles) will be used for the shrouds

Competitors in the Half-Ton Cup championship enter Portsmouth Harbour at the end of a day's sailing off Hayling Island.

and forestay, but hydraulic rams are commonly fitted to the backstay, so that the tension can be adjusted to suit a particular point of sailing.

Sails are now made of Terylene, but may have to be renewed half-way through a season as they will have lost their original shape and, therefore, their full efficiency as the source of power. A mainsail can easily cost as much as a car.

In order to haul up the sails and keep their luffs tight, and, once they are up, control their sheeting, hand-winches are fitted to be worked by the crew. On even an average ocean racer, twelve winches are the minimum required. In some cases these are linked together so that to achieve extra power more than one person can winch at a time. The rules state that everything on the boat must be manually operated, so the winches are a very vital part of a racing yacht's equipment. The gear ratios on a sheet winch can reach up to 72 to 1 and on larger boats, where even more power is required, an even more powerful winch is often fitted—known as a *coffee-grinder* because of its re-

semblance to old-fashioned hand-operated grinders. Even so, when a boat is short tacking, in other words tacking frequently, the winchmen will have to be relieved after half a dozen tacks.

The navigation instruments carried compare with an aeroplane for complexity and cost. An electric echosounder will indicate the exact depth of water beneath the boat. A log will record the nautical miles covered and show the speed at which the boat is travelling. In order to ensure that the boat is achieving her maximum speed, an amplified log is usually fitted as well. This is an instrument that has an adjustable centre so that the needle is placed in the middle for a chosen speed. The clock is then divided either way in one-tenths of knots and if the boat fractionally loses or gains speed, the instrument will indicate it.

A radio direction finder (RDF) is the instrument used to obtain a radio bearing from radio beacons scattered around the coast. These beacons transmit identification signals in morse code, for instance the one at Cape Finisterre transmits

two dashes followed by a long single note. As the navigator rotates the direction-finder, this note will rise and fall and by reading the bearing when the lowest note (null) is reached, the navigator has the bearing of his boat from the radio beacon.

In order to make the best use of sails, the skipper needs to know the wind direction and speed. At the top of the mast where the cleanest wind is to be found, an anemometer and wind vane are fitted. These are wired up to dials in the cockpit and indicate both the relative wind speed and direction. They cannot indicate the true wind speed and direction as the boat's movement through the water creates a relative effect. In a modern ocean-racing yacht, tuning up occupies many weeks of the hard training before the racing season commences.

With all the instruments now available the crew no longer rely upon their "seat of pants" feelings for achieving the optimum performance, as the effect of a slight adjustment can be noticed quickly on the instruments. Many yachts have now taken this a stage further and fitted small analogue computers which give an indication of their performance by providing a constant readout of the ratio between the boat's speed through the water and the wind strength. The use of these computers when actually racing is forbidden, but they provide useful tuning information.

Ocean racing is not a cheap sport. At the end of the season, unless the boat has been particularly successful, it will be worth nothing like as much as it cost. But while the owners have to be wealthy, the crews come from all walks of life, drawing to yachting a spread of background and experience that is perhaps unique in sport.

Opposite above: Sayula (Mexico). Winner of the 1973 Round the World Race.

Opposite below: the crew of the British newspaper proprietor, Sir Max Aitken's yacht Perseverance *working the coffee-grinder.*

Above: Class IV and V boats. Boat classifications allow for well organized races.

CHAPTER 6

THE AMERICA'S CUP

Despite the growing attraction of ocean racing, and the prestige and publicity that surrounds the Olympics, the America's Cup is still the most prestigious international yachting event. The fact that to launch and support a challenge or defence for the cup costs a vast amount of money means that races for it are infrequently staged. This increases the excitement among yachtsmen when a race does occur. In one respect the cup is unique. Ever since the 100 Guineas Cup presented by Queen Victoria for a race round the Isle of Wight was won by the American Schooner *America* in 1851, no other country has won, and the cup still rests in the clubhouse of the New York Yacht Club. No less than twenty challenges have been made since 1851 but only on a couple of occasions has the challenger come near to winning despite the confident claims made before the actual race.

Nowadays, the races are sailed in 12 metre yachts—large, open cockpit day boats of about 23 metres (70 feet) in length. But in earlier years, the race was between yachts of very dissimilar design and rig and there was no handicap system to equate them. This is perhaps as well, as had there been a handicap system in 1851 the *America* would have been beaten in the first race by the much smaller English yacht *Aurora* which finished only 21 minutes later, and we would have had no America's Cup today. The first race came about as the result of an invitation by the Earl of Wilton, Commodore of the Royal Yacht Squadron, which wished to stage races in the Solent to celebrate the Great Exhibition of 1851. The *America* was sailed across the Atlantic, and on the way to Cowes

Opposite: Gretel, *the Australian challenger for the America's Cup, in final trials off Sydney Heads.*

The schooner America.

Top: Livonia, *James Ashbury's challenger for the Cup in 1871.*

Bottom: Dauntless *and* Cambria *racing for the Cup in 1870.*

was met by the British yacht *Laverock* which she soundly beat, so much so that British yachts were chary of racing against her thereafter. In those days most races were accompanied by considerable side-betting, and no one likes betting on a certain loser. The Round the Island Race took place on 22 August against the top British boats of the time, the fastest of which unfortunately went aground, and the *America* won the cup. The syndicate who owned her sold her in England and returned to New York with the cup. In 1857 the Syndicate decided to offer the cup to the New York Yacht Club as a permanent challenge trophy, with certain conditions.

New York, July 8, 1857

To the Secretary of the New York Yacht Club:

Sir,

The undersigned, members of the New York Yacht Club, and later owners of the schooner yacht AMERICA, beg leave through you to present the Club the Cup won by the AMERICA at the Regatta of the Royal Yacht Squadron at Cowes, England, August 22, 1851.

This cup was offered as a prize to be sailed for by yachts of all nations without regard to difference of tonnage, going round the Isle of Wight, the usual course for the Annual Regatta of the Royal Yacht Squadron, and was won by the AMERICA, beating eight cutters and seven schooner yachts which started in the race.

The Cup is offered to the New York Yacht Club, subject to the following conditions:

Any organised Yacht Club of any foreign country shall always be entitled, through any one or more of its members to claim the right of sailing a match for this Cup with any yacht or other vessel of not less than 30 or more than 300 tons, measured by the Custom House rule of the country to which the vessel belongs. The parties desiring to sail for the Cup may make any match with the Yacht Club in possession of the same that may be determined upon by mutual consent, but in case of disagreement as to terms, the match shall be sailed over the usual course for the Annual Regatta of the Yacht Club in possession of the Cup, and subject to the Rules and Sailing Regulations, the challenging party being bound to give six months' notice in writing, fixing the day on which they wish to start. This notice to embrace the length, Custom House measurement, rig and name of vessel. It is to be distinctly understood that the Cup is to be the property of the Club, and not of the members thereof, or owners of the vessels winning it in a match; and that the condition of keeping it open to be sailed for by Yacht Clubs of all foreign countries, upon the terms above laid down, shall forever attach to it, thus making it a perpetual Challenge Cup for friendly competition between foreign countries.

> J. C. STEVENS
> EDWIN A. STEVENS
> HAMILTON WILKES
> J. BEEKMAN FINLAY
> GEORGE L. SCHUYLER

Some of the details have changed, but the principles of the challenge have not changed to date.

The first challenges

Unfortunately, no one expressed an immediate interest in the cup, and it was not until 1868 that the first challenge was issued by James Ashbury, the Vice-Commodore of the Royal Harwich Yacht Club in England. His challenge invited the New York Yacht Club to send their fastest boat over to Europe for the season, after which he would race it back across the Atlantic in his schooner *Cambria* for a wager of £250 ($500), and then the two boats would sail three races for the cup. A long correspondence ensued, while Ashbury tried to have centre-board boats excluded from the challenge in which he was not ultimately successful.

In 1870, however, *Cambria* raced *Dauntless*, a crack American yacht that had been sailing in Europe at the time, across the Atlantic and beat her by 1 hour and 43 minutes. *Cambria*'s time for the crossing was 23 days, 5 hours and 17 minutes.

Only one race took place for the cup and *Cambria* found herself sailing against 23 American yachts. The Americans gave *Cambria* the windward end of the start line which was the advantageous position, but just before the start the wind changed and *Cambria* found herself at the leeward end of the line, her sail blanketed by the American boats. She finished eighth. Among the American boats was the original *America*, now back under her original flag, which finished fourth.

Ashbury did not take his defeat lying down and immediately upon his return to England ordered a new schooner *Livonia* and challenged again. This time it was arranged that the challenger should race against only one defending yacht in the best of seven races, but the Americans reserved the right to race one of four defenders, the defending yacht to be nominated each day.

The first race took place on 16 October, 1871 and was won by the defender *Columbia* which also sailed and won the second race. *Livonia* won the third race when *Columbia*'s steering failed and the Americans nominated *Sappho* which won the fourth and fifth races.

After the fifth race the Americans claimed a victory, but Ashbury had threatening to bring a lawyer if he challenged again, but in the event he looked for challenge elsewhere and became a Member of Parliament.

Livonia, incidentally, had the largest sail area of any yacht in the history of the cup, having enough canvas to cover more than six tennis courts!

The English lost interest after Ashbury's second defeat, but five years later, in 1876, a Royal

The Countess of Dufferin, *Canada's 1876 challenger.*

protested that in the second race he had left a mark of the course to starboard, which meant he had to gybe round it, while *Columbia* had left it to port which entailed a much quicker tack, and as a result *Livonia* had lost considerable ground. Had this been the case the score would have been three to two. Ashbury claimed that under the Royal Yacht Squadron rules of the time, if the side of the mark was not specified it should be left to starboard. The New York Yacht Club ruled that it was optional and thus the 'cup was retained by America.

Ashbury returned to Britain

Canadian Yacht Club Syndicate headed by the Vice-Commodore, Major Charles Gifford, challenged with a centreboard schooner, the *Countess of Dufferin*, stipulating that the single defender should be named before the racing. The Americans agreed and entered the schooner *Madeleine* which was an easy winner.

The *Countess of Dufferin* syndicate ran short of money before the end of the series, and their yacht was sold to satisfy creditors. The largest shareholder Alexander Cuthbert tried again, however, in 1881 with his cutter *Atalanta* designed and built by himself. He ran into the sort of troubles that beset boat-owners today, however, and his boat was finished late. To save time he sailed her down the Erie Canal to New York, quite a feat in itself. The *Atalanta* had a full amateur crew which was something of a novelty in those days, but they proved no match for the defending sloop *Mischief*. The owner of *Mischief* was in fact an Englishman, J. B. Busk, who was a New York Yacht Club member. It is ironic that the only time an English-owned yacht has ever won a Cup Series, she was sailing for the defenders.

After the fourth challenge the New York Yacht Club asked the only surviving member of the original America Syndicate to change the deeds of gift. The changes included the addition of a clause that the challenger would have to meet any one yacht, and not a selection as had been the case for James Ashbury. The Canadians were particularly affected by two other clauses—one of these stipulated that the challenger had to sail to the races, which effectively stopped any challengers coming down the Erie Canal. The other was even more direct and said that the challenging club had to hold its annual regatta on the sea which eliminated further challenges from the Great Lakes. The other important clause stipulated that the challenging yacht had to be built in the country she was going to represent.

"Genesta", "Galatea" and the "Thistle"

Two challenges were made in 1884 from England, and the Committee ruled that Sir Richard Sutton's *Genesta* should race in 1885, and if she failed then Lieutenant William Henn's *Galatea* should race in 1886.

In the first race, in 1885, the American defender *Puritan*, while on the port tack, was hit fair and square by *Genesta* which was on starboard tack. The Committee immediately disqualified *Puritan* for failing to give way. Sir Richard, in a sporting gesture that shines out in the history of the cup, refused to cross the line and insisted that the race be abandoned. In the second race *Genesta* started at the leeward

Galatea *the 1886 challenger skippered by David Bradford.* Galatea *was defeated by* Mayflower.

end of the line and never recovered, losing by 16 minutes. The third race was much closer and at the half-way mark *Genesta* was ahead. She appears to have carried too much canvas on her return leg, however, and *Puritan* narrowly beat her home.

As the series was the best of three, the fifth challenge ended with the cup still with the New York Yacht Club.

Galatea had a poor season in 1885, and lost all her races to the *Mayflower* owned by General Paine. Lieutenant Henn accepted his defeat gracefully and bowed out of the cup. If nothing else, he and Sir Richard Sutton contributed to a general raising of the standards of sportsmanship and interest of the cup.

In 1887 close on the heels of *Galatea*, the Scots, in the form of a Royal Clyde Yacht Club syndicate, arrived with *Thistle* which was designed to suit a new British rating which no longer penalized width. So, unlike the previous challengers, *Thistle* was comparatively beamy. She had a good season in European waters winning eleven of the fifteen races she entered, and then sailed across to New York in 22 days. The New York Yacht Club chose *Volunteer*, a large centreboard yacht again owned by General Paine, which won both races in light and fresh conditions. The Scots complained about the course which they said favoured local knowledge. This complaint could easily have been made by the *America* in 1851 and the answer was to spend more time racing in the cup-holder's waters to gain local knowledge.

The Earl of Dunraven and the "Valkyries"

The eighth challenge came from the Earl of Dunraven through the Royal Yacht Squadron in 1893. The challenging boat, *Valkyrie II*, was sleek and fast, and the Americans chose the fastest boat they had, *Vigilant*, to defend. These two boats looked much more like modern racing boats than any of the yachts in the previous races.

The first race on 5 October, 1893 was abandoned for lack of wind after *Valkyrie II* was leading at the outer mark by 25 minutes. This was by far the most impressive performance of any challenger so far, and the Americans realized that they had a real fight on their hands. In the next race the Americans came out determined to pick up and after

a hard-fought race won by 7 minutes—a good margin.

The weather for the third race provided a good fresh breeze and *Vigilant* took the lead at the start to lead by five minutes at the end of the first leg. Two reaches remained to the finish and try as she could, *Valkyrie II* could not close the gap; so the Americans took a two-race lead.

The fourth race provided really strong winds, so much that *Vigilant*'s designer Nat G. Herreshoff took the helm as the professional skipper refused to take the boat out. *Valkyrie II* led at the end of the first leg and then set her spinnaker for the run. Unfortunately, it was torn while being hoisted and soon blew out. A light-weather spinnaker suffered the same fate and a balloon jib was set topsail as a spinnaker. For some unaccountable reason, she did not set her largest topsail or shake out the reefs in the mainsail.

The Americans had more success in setting their spinnaker and they also set just about everything else they had for the run home in a near gale. The result was one of the most exciting and closely fought finishes in cup history, with the defender slowly creeping up on the challenger to win by 40 seconds.

Two years later Lord Dunraven returned with *Valkyrie III*, a boat designed on American lines, and the first to be designed purely for the America's Cup. She did not perform well against *Britannia* losing two out of three races, but *Britannia* had beaten *Vigilant* in twelve out of seventeen races, so on average at least *Valkyrie III* appeared to be as good as *Vigilant*. C. Oliver Iselin again led a syndicate which built the appropriately named *Defender*, designed by Nat Herreshoff but based rather upon the lines of *Valkyrie II*.

Such an interchange of ideas should hopefully have led to increased harmony in the series. Unfortunately, due to faults on both sides, the ninth challenge was one of the most unhappy.

The first race was won by *Defender* but Lord Dunraven claimed that *Valkyrie III* had been hampered by the spectator fleet. The New York Yacht Club agreed and promised to try to keep the spectators clear in the subsequent races. Lord Dunraven's second complaint was much more serious, in that it suggested that the Americans had added ballast during the night. The boats were measured and found to be floating at their original pre-race waterlines, but Lord Dunraven insisted that he had seen the ballast being put on board and the suspicion poisoned the remainder of the series. The wrangling continued long after the series and as Lord Dunraven refused to withdraw his allegation he was eventually expelled from the New York Yacht Club. Subsequently, the defenders admitted that they *had* moved ballast during the night in question, but only to remove large pigs of iron ballast that did not fit properly so as to cut them into smaller more manageable sizes. The whole unfortunate business might have been avoided if this had been admitted right at the beginning.

In the second race *Valkyrie III* crossed the finish line first, but already the poison created by the ballast issue was having its effect. Despite the efforts of the New York Yacht Club, a large steamer got between the boats at the start, and *Valkyrie III* fouled *Defender*, breaking her topmast stay. *Valkyrie III* did not stop and was subsequently disqualified. Lord Dunraven again complained about the spectator fleet, and the Committee agreed to keep the start clear, but said they could

not guarantee to keep the course clear. Dunraven replied that he would only race if the Committee would declare the race void if either of the competitors was hindered by the spectator fleet. If the Committee refused, *Valkyrie III* would cross the line to give *Defender* the race and then retire. The Committee did not receive the last message until after the start, when *Valkyrie III* crossed the line, then immediately hauled down her racing flag and returned to her moorings.

Both sides must share the blame for the unfortunate result of the ninth challenge, as with hindsight, we can see that the arguments built up as a result of small seemingly insignificant events during the course of the series. It is easy to criticize now, but both syndicates and crews must have been under considerable tension at the time of this particular series.

Sir Thomas Lipton

In 1899 the most famous of all challengers appeared on the scene, the man who was to dominate the cup for the next 32 years. This was Sir Thomas Lipton, a self-made millionaire who had built up his fortune as a tea merchant. He had been knighted in 1898 and was made a baronet in 1902. Prejudice in English society was still strongly against ennobled tradesmen at the end of the 19th century and although Sir Thomas was a personal friend of the Prince of Wales, he was only made a member of the Royal Yacht Squadron in 1931, just before he died.

As a result the challenge was made by the Royal Ulster Yacht Club, and the boat was christened *Shamrock*. William Fife, the designer, built her with a light displacement which was in line with

Lord Dunraven's frustration at the spectator fleet can be well understood from this view of Valkyrie III *racing against* Defender *in 1895.*

the current American racing rules, and the hull was made of manganese bronze below the waterline with aluminium topsides of 42 metres (128 feet) over all. She set 1,243 square metres (13,492 square feet) of sail.

Iselin again lead the defending syndicate, his third defence, with the American financier J. Pierpont Morgan. Nat Herreshoff once again designed and built the yacht, called *Columbia*. This experienced American combination made short work of the series, winning all three races. The series was, however, a great success. More spectator boats than ever came to observe the racing, but this time they were kept out of the way of the competitors throughout the race by the U.S. Navy. Lipton was a gallant and graceful loser and did a great deal to raise the status of the America's Cup.

Undeterred by his defeat, Sir Thomas challenged again in 1901 with a new *Shamrock* designed by George L. Watson who had produced *Thistle* and the *Valkyries*. *Shamrock II* was one of the earliest boats to have her design extensively tank tested, and she appeared to be a very fast boat. At the beginning of the season she was not as fast as the first *Shamrock*, but improved each time she was sailed.

The Americans again chose *Columbia* to defend, which gave the challenger their best chance for years. The races were very close, the challenger coming closer each time until she lost by only 41 seconds in the third race. Once again the Americans had successfully defended the cup.

Two years later Lipton was back again with *Shamrock III* designed by William Fife. Although *Shamrock I* was available as a trial horse, so that the new boat could be properly tuned before the series, she never stood a chance. Nat Herreshoff designed—for a syndicate of New York millionaires—a new boat called *Reliance*, a sloop of 44 metres (143 feet) length. She won all three races and *Shamrock III* did not even finish the last race as she became lost in fog.

Sir Thomas challenged again in 1907 but on the condition that both boats should be built to the new American Universal Rule and of identical length. Up until this time the America's Cup races had always been run on a time-allowance handicap system, but in the early part of the 20th century the Americans adopted the Universal Rule while the International Rule was adopted in Europe. The Americans refused the challenge and another on similar terms in 1912. Sir Thomas made an unconditional challenge in 1913 which was immediately accepted. The Universal Rule was chosen

although the Americans reserved the right to decide their waterline length. This meant that time allowance had still to be applied.

Shamrock IV was designed by Charles E. Nicholson and although designed to the Universal Rule she had a typically English look about her. The defender, owned by Cornelius Vanderbilt, was once again designed by Nat Herreshoff and was christened *Resolute*. World War I broke out when *Shamrock IV* was half-way across the Atlantic and on arrival in New York she was laid up for the duration of the war.

In 1920 the challenge was renewed and *Shamrock IV* and *Resolute* were tuned up in readiness. The gun went for the first race and *Shamrock IV* was slightly over the line but she soon recovered. Both boats got into difficulties at the first mark and *Resolute* which had lost her throat halyard, withdrew leaving *Shamrock*

IV to become the first challenger to win a race since *Livonia* 49 years before.

Shamrock IV won the second race and for the first time ever a challenger looked as if it had a chance of winning the cup. The third race was very close. *Resolute* led at the mark, but *Shamrock IV* overhauled her on the last leg and crossed the line first. Unfortunately, she was not far enough ahead to make up for the time allowance, and *Resolute* was the winner on handicap. This win seemed to encourage the Americans who won both the following races and retained the cup, but it had been a closely fought series.

In the next few years agreement was reached upon the adoption of a class rating for the America's Cup races, and eventually the Universal J Class Rule was chosen. The rating was found by taking 18 per cent of the waterline, which had to be

Atalanta *and* Mischief *sail for the Cup in 1881.*

between 21 and 27 metres (70 and 87 feet), multiplying it by the square root of the sail area in square feet and then in cubic feet, so that the answers equalled 23 metres (76 feet). This may seem complicated but it is simple arithmetic compared with later rating formulas, and it did at least mean that at last there was no handicap to be worked out, the first boat across the finish line would be the winner.

No challenge was made for ten years after the thirteenth series, but then in 1930 Sir Thomas Lipton challenged again. His boat, still called *Shamrock* and the fifth of the name, was designed by Charles E. Nicholson. The Americans built no fewer than four possible defenders, *Yankee, Weetamoe, Whirlwind* and *Enterprise*, and a series of trials was organized to decide which yacht should defend the cup. After some hard-fought races *Enterprise* emerged as the fastest boat. These trials undoubtedly gave the defender an advantage over the challenger, as the actual trial races provided conditions identical to the race series itself. *Enterprise* was a considerable step ahead of most boats of the day, her mast was made of duralumin and weighed only two-thirds of *Shamrock V*'s wooden mast. Her boom was triangular and her winches the last word in mechanical efficiency. She cost five times as much as *Shamrock V*.

The cup series was to be the best of seven, and in the first race, despite poor navigation and being caught unfavourably by a wind shift, *Enterprise* won by three minutes which gave an indication of her superior speed and tuning.

The second race was a repeat but *Enterprise* won by over nine minutes. On the third race *Shamrock V* broke her main halyard and withdrew. On the fourth race, as if to

get the whole thing over, *Enterprise* won by nearly six minutes, and the only morsel of comfort to the challenger was that it made up three minutes after the first mark of the triangular course. *Enterprise*, incidentally, broke the course record during the race. This was Sir Thomas Lipton's last attempt, as he died in 1931 at the age of 82. No one has tried harder or more sportingly to win the "auld mug". He dominated the cup for over 30 years, longer than anyone else. He built more yachts and made more challenges, and more than anyone else built the America's Cup into a legend.

The "Endeavours'" attempts

For a while after Sir Thomas Lipton's death, it seemed doubtful if there would be another challenge. *Shamrock V*, however, was sold to Tom Sopwith (later Sir Thomas), the aircraft manufacturer, and in

1932 she was the most successful of the English J Class boats. After this success, Sopwith took the next logical step and issued a challenge for 1934 which was accepted. He built a new J Class yacht, designed by Charles E. Nicholson and christened *Endeavour*. She was an immediately successful boat and hopes rose for a successful challenge at last. Unfortunately, on the eve of her departure for the United States, her professional crew went on strike for higher wages. Sopwith replaced them with amateurs, but there was no time for crew-training in pre-series races.

Meanwhile, a new American boat *Rainbow*, owned by the American railway millionaire W. S. Vanderbilt, won the selection series to defend the cup. Once again the series was to be the best of seven. The first race took place on 15 September, but had to be abandoned, because of lack of wind, when *Rainbow* was leading

Endeavour by round about a mile.

At first the second race, the first to count, looked to be a repeat, in that *Rainbow* quickly took the lead. Once Sopwith tacked for the mark, however, *Endeavour* really began to move and although she set her spinnaker late finally overtook the defender to win by 2 minutes and 9 seconds. On the second race to count there was a fresh breeze and *Endeavour* sailed straight through *Rainbow*'s lee. The two boats remained locked together for the next eight miles, but on the beat *Endeavour* opened up a gap. On the last leg *Rainbow* began to catch up as *Endeavour* had to set a balloon jib because her genoa had been torn. *Endeavour* hung on to her lead, however, to win by 57 seconds in a new record time for the course.

Endeavour took the lead at the start of the third race, and was still leading by the beginning of the final leg when the wind fell. For some unaccountable reason, instead of making straight for the finish line which he could have done, Sopwith tacked to cover *Rainbow*. In the ensuing duel he lost out tactically and *Rainbow* won by 3 minutes and 25 seconds. There is a rule in racing, that if you are clear of the other boat and can sail for the mark, then you just sail straight for it. The only reason for covering an opponent, or keeping closely between him and the mark, is if you have to tack towards it or the winds are variable. Neither applied in this case.

The fourth race was spoilt by arguments. First *Rainbow* caught *Endeavour* on the starboard tack and a near collision occurred. Next, as the two boats came up to the first mark *Endeavour* luffed *Rainbow* which failed to respond. On the advice of the New York Yacht Club observer on board Sopwith did not immediately hoist his protest

Sceptre, *the 12-metre yacht which challenged for the Cup for the UK in 1958. She is pictured here at Poole in Dorset on the south coast of England while on trial before setting sail for the U.S.*

did better off the start, but hung on to her genoa too long in the rising wind so that *Rainbow* slipped past her. On the last leg, with *Rainbow* still slightly ahead, the challenger began to gain rapidly and once again Sopwith threw away the race by insisting on covering his opponent instead of heading for the line. The Americans took full advantage of this and steered a course to leeward of the line, luffing up towards it when about a mile away. *Rainbow* went better harder on the wind and won by 55 seconds.

Like the series before, the fifteenth series had been closely fought. *Endeavour* had proved herself the faster boat, but she had had a comparatively inexperienced crew and her skipper made two tactical errors that cost him the only real chance a challenger had ever had of winning the cup.

Like others before him, once bitten by the bug Sopwith could not resist another attempt, and two years later he launched *Endeavour II* for the sixteenth challenge in 1937. Like her predecessor, she was designed by Charles E. Nicholson, but she was designed to the maximum waterline length allowed in J Class boats and had a heavier displacement.

In the United States there was considerable concern at this new challenge. *Endeavour I* had come close to beating *Rainbow* and no one could be found to build the new defender which was undoubtedly required. Eventually another of the fabulously wealthy Vanderbilts ordered a new boat, designed by Olin Stephens after exhaustive tank tests and christened *Ranger*. She was found on trials to be very much faster than the other American J Class boats and was selected as the defender. Unlike previous challengers, Sopwith took both *Endeavours* across the Atlantic

flag, waiting instead until near the finish. The New York Yacht Club subsequently refused to hear his protest on the grounds that he should have hoisted his protest flag immediately after the incident. In the end neither protest was heard, and *Rainbow* won by 1 minute and 25 seconds.

In the fifth race, benefiting from a balloon spinnaker loaned from another boat, the defender for the first time went faster off the wind than the challenger, and in spite of tearing this same spinnaker and losing and recovering a man overside, won by 4 minutes, the largest margin of the series.

If the Americans won the next race, the cup would remain in the New York Yacht Club. *Endeavour*

and held his own trials to decide which of his boats would challenge. *Endeavour II* established herself as the faster of the two. It looked like being an exciting series, as both the boats were faster than those in the previous series, but in fact it was a great disappointment as *Ranger* trounced the challenger in four straight races.

Ranger was in fact a remarkable boat and way ahead of any other J Class boat afloat. But the class was dying because of the high cost and the Js never raced again after 1937.

The 12 metre Class

World War II brought an end to the most active racing for the cup since it was first put up for competition. But even when *Ranger* and *Endeavour* were racing it was realized that the enormous cost of the J Class yachts was going to force the rules to be changed to allow a smaller craft to be used in future if the competition were to continue.

In 1956 the rules were amended and the 12 metre Class was designed for future races. At the same time it was specified that the future challengers and defenders must be designed and built in the country they were to represent.

Twelve metre yachts are not boats of 12 metres, or roughly 40 feet, in length, they are boats built to the following formula:

$$\frac{L + 2D + \sqrt{SA - F}}{2.37} = 12 \text{ metres}$$

Where   L = corrected length 17.5 centimetres (7 inches) above the waterline
  D = skin girth minus chain girth
  SA = mainsail plus 85% fore triangle
  F = freeboard.

As soon as the new rules were agreed the Royal Yacht Squadron of England issued a challenge for 1958. The British boat, named *Sceptre* and designed by David Boyd was built for a syndicate and launched on 1 April. The Americans built three new boats *Columbia*, *Weatherly* and *Easterner* and also had the very successful *Vim* from which to choose the defender. After an intensive series of elimination races *Columbia* designed by Olin Stephens proved herself the best boat and was chosen to defend the cup. The series proved that the Americans still held a convincing lead in design. In the first race *Columbia* came home 7 minutes and 44 seconds ahead of *Sceptre* after leading from the start. Not only did the defender move better through the water but her sails looked far superior.

The second race was sailed in a strong breeze and was won by *Columbia* with a margin of 12 minutes, one of the largest for a long time.

Although the gap was narrowed to 8 minutes in the third race and 7 minutes in the fourth, *Sceptre* was never really in the running and would probably have lost to any one of the four American boats.

Despite the American walkover, the series attracted a tremendous amount of interest and two other nations expressed an interest in challenging, with the Australians getting in first with a challenge from the Royal Sydney Yacht Club for a syndicate lead by Sir Frank Packer. Their boat *Gretel* designed by Alan Payne worked up against *Vim* which was bought from the Americans to act as a trial horse.

After extensive trials, the Americans chose a modified *Weatherly* sailed by Bus Mosbacher to defend the cup. The first race took place in blustery conditions, in which *Gretel* broke some of her rigging and as a result lost the race. In the second race the wind was even stronger and unhampered by damaged rigging the Australian boat seemed much happier. Although *Weatherly* lead at the last mark of the course, *Gretel* was first up with her spinnaker for the run home and sailed past the defender to win by 47 seconds to a rapturous reception. This was the first victory by a challenging yacht for 28 years. Brim-full of confidence after their victory, the Australians put up a good fight in the third race but the conditions were light and variable and seemed to suit the defender admirably. In these sort of conditions it takes more than skill and concentration to win—luck with the wind shifts counts for a great deal and Mosbacher had the luck and won by nearly 9 minutes. On the fourth race *Weatherly* took the lead at the start of what turned out to be a hard-tacking duel. One boat will have an advantageous position as far as wind and the two boats' relative positions are concerned— by constantly following as the other boat tacks, she can sit to weather, or up wind on her and hold the position between the other boat and the mark of the course, thereby guaranteeing to pass the mark first. This is hard physical work for the crews and calls for a skipper's undivided concentration. The two boats were neck and neck at the finish but *Weatherly* crossed the line first by 26 seconds. Mosbacher had only to win the fifth race to clinch the defence and indeed he took an early lead and hung on to it.

So ended the eighteenth challenge which was closer than the final score of 4 to 1 indicated. The Australians had bustled in as new boys to the competition, but their showing was more than creditable.

In 1964 the British challenged again with another David Boyd design for Tony Boyden, called *Sovereign*. Another new British boat was available as a possible contender, *Kurrewa V*, also a Boyd design. Trials were arranged to take place off Newport, Rhode Island, where the actual racing would take place, so as to give experience to the crews. Peter Scott, the British naturalist and an experienced dinghy helmsman, was chosen to skipper *Sovereign*. The Americans again held selection races and *Constellation* skippered by Bob Bavier Jnr won the right to defend.

The series was a walkover for the Americans who won the first four races, the second by the incredible margin of over 20 minutes. There was considerable criticism of Scott in Britain after the series, but *Sovereign* was outdesigned and could never sail as close to the wind as *Constellation*.

Sir Frank Packer, leader of the syndicate that owned Gretel *and* Dame Pattie.

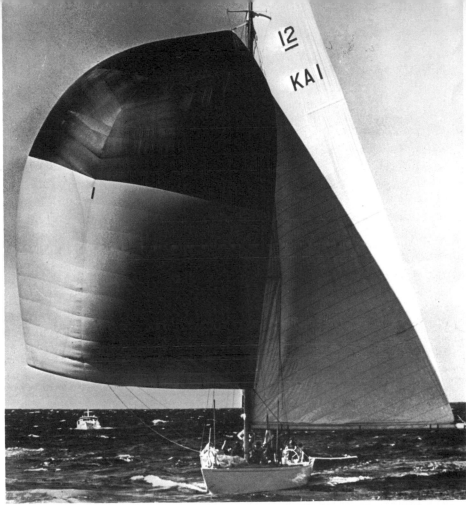

Gretel.

Dame Pattie.

Three years later Sir Frank Packer was back again for the Australians with a new 12 metre called *Dame Pattie*. This time Bus Mosbacher with *Intrepid* was the defender and he made short work of the series, winning four straight races. The Australians were never beaten by as large a margin as *Sovereign* but they seemed to lack the spirit which was a feature of their first challenge and

Southern Cross.

after losing the first race their morale declined. Undaunted by this defeat, however, the Australians quickly put in another challenge for 1970. France, Britain and Greece also challenged, and in order to stimulate the competition, the New York Yacht Club suggested that all four challengers should take part in an elimination series and the winner of this would be selected as the ultimate challenger for 1970. The challenging countries agreed to this novel but imaginative suggestion, but by 1970 the British and Greek challenges had been withdrawn and the choice lay between France and Australia. The elimination races were close. The Australian boat *Gretel II*, helmed by Jim Hardy, eventually won, due as much as anything to the constant changing of the helmsmen aboard the French entry *France*, but the racing was close.

The Americans chose *Intrepid* skippered by Bill Ficker to defend the cup. The Australian boat soon showed superior sailing ability and it looked as if the American design superiority had been caught up at last. But the Americans still held the superiority in skill and Ficker managed to hold off what became the closest challenge since *Endeavour* in 1934. Unfortunately, the series was marred by a protest by the Americans at the start of the second race which was upheld by the Race Committee, quite correctly in fact, but it created an unfortunate atmosphere redolent of Dunraven and Sopwith.

Undeterred, however, the Australians challenged again for 1974 with a Bob Miller-designed 12 metre christened *Southern Cross* which worked up against *Gretel II*. She quickly disposed of *France* which had also challenged and then faced *Courageous* the winner of the American elimination races, and which was skippered by Ted Hood.

Southern Cross seemed to be a fast boat, but the American elimination races gave the defenders an unmatchable advantage as far as crew-training and tactical practice was concerned. The *Courageous* won four straight races and the cup remained bolted firmly to its table in the New York Yacht Club. Further challenges are in the pipe-line, but the high cost and limited use of 12 metre yachts, is once again bringing up the question of the type of boat to be used in cup competition. The most sensible alternative being discussed is the use of IOR ocean-racing yachts to a fixed rating which would allow a large number of countries to challenge with boats that have a wider use.

Sceptre *just before she acted as a trial horse against* Kurrewa II.

CHAPTER 7

THE OLYMPIC CLASSES

Sailing was not included as an Olympic sport until the French Games in 1900, when Britain won three Golds, France two, and Germany and the U.S. one each.

For the modern Olympics, six classes of boats are chosen from among the many keel boats and dinghies sailed internationally. Each nation can enter one boat in each class and the competition consists of seven races. Points are awarded each position at the end of each race, the winner receiving no points, the second—3 points, third—5.7, fourth—8, fifth—10, sixth—11.7, seventh—13, eighth—14, ninth—15, tenth—16, and so on. After seven races have been completed each competitor discards his worst performance and the Gold Medal goes to the boat that then has the fewest points. Silver and Bronze Medals are awarded to the next two boats. Thus each nation can only win six sailing medals.

In the 1972 Olympics in Germany six classes chosen were the Finn, a single-handed dinghy, the Tempest and Star, both two-handed keel boats, the Flying Dutchman, a two-handed dinghy, and the Soling and Dragon, three-handed keelers.

The Star

The class with the greatest seniority as an Olympic boat was the Star which originated in the United States in 1910 as a cheap gaff-rigged racing boat designed by Francis Sweisguth. It first appeared as an Olympic boat in the 1932 Olympics at Los Angeles and has been sailed ever since. During the years the Star Class has kept pace with the latest developments and construction techniques. In 1921 the gaff rig was replaced by the Bermudan rig and in 1929 the present-day 9.8 metre (32 foot) mast was introduced. The Star Class was swift to adopt glass-reinforced plastics as a material for the hulls and was in the forefront of the development of the "bendy mast", "compulsory buoyancy" and "toe straps".

At Kiel in 1972 the Australians won the Gold, Sweden the Silver and Germany the Bronze. This was the Star's last appearance in the Olympics. The International Olympic Committee decided after Kiel that the Star was to be replaced, but it is difficult to believe that the strong fleets still sailing in the United States, Sweden and other countries will abandon their class so quickly.

The Dragon

The largest of the Olympic boats was the Dragon, a three-man boat which also had its last Olympic competition in 1972. The Dragon

Flying Dutchman, Olympic class, with spinnaker reaching.

Star
Length 6.9 m. 22.66 ft.
Draught 1.0 m. 3.25 ft.
Keel weight 408 kilos.
900 lb.
Minimum all up weight
662 kilos. 1460 lb.
Sail area 27 sq. m.
285 sq. ft.

Dragon
Length 8.9 m. 29.17 ft.
Beam 1.9 m. 6.75 ft.
Draught 1.3 m. 4.17 ft.
Displacement 1700 kilos.
3747 lbs.
Keel weight 207 kilos.
460 lb.
Sail area 30 sq. m.
286 sq. ft.

Soling
Length 8.5 m. 26.75 ft.
Beam 1.9 m. 6.25 ft.
Draught 1.3 m. 4.25 ft.
Displacement 997.9 kilos.
2200 lb.
Keel weight 580.6 kilos.
1280 lb.
Sail area 21.5 sq. m.
233 sq. ft.

was designed in Norway in 1929 by Johan Anker as a one-design within the 20 square metre Class. Theoretically all the boats are the same as it was originally intended to be a small cheap boat in which two or three people could sail comfortably. A small cabin was provided in case an occasional night on board proved necessary. The cabin no longer exists except as a small shelter for the crew but the class still insists that a token coach roof be built on deck. It is interesting to compare the difference between the over-all length and waterline length of the Dragon Class with the similar measurements of more modern boats. In modern boats the difference is almost negligible, showing the modern trend to gain the maximum waterline length in a particular hull and thus the maximum speed.

The Soling

A new boat in 1972 was the three-man keel boat, the Soling, designed by the Norwegian Jan Herman Linge in 1963. The class received international status in 1967 and was selected by the International Olympic Committee to replace the 5.5 metre (18 foot) class at Kiel.

As the Soling is one of the newest boats to be chosen for the Olympics it is interesting to look at the development programme from the boat's first inception to its final acceptance. In 1962 the IYRU decided to have a new international three-man keel-boat class of roughly the same size as the 5.5 metre (18 foot). Linge, who was already working on the design for a slightly smaller boat which, using glass-reinforced plastic (GRP) for its construction, should halve the cost of a 5.5 metre, suggested a lighter boat but the Committee left the decision open. In 1963 Linge had his plans ready and found a boat-yard prepared to finance the project and a wooden prototype was built which was evaluated during 1964. As a result of these trials it was decided to go ahead with the production of a mould from the proto-type and a first run of five GRP boats was constructed in time for the 1966 season.

The IYRU held trials for the new

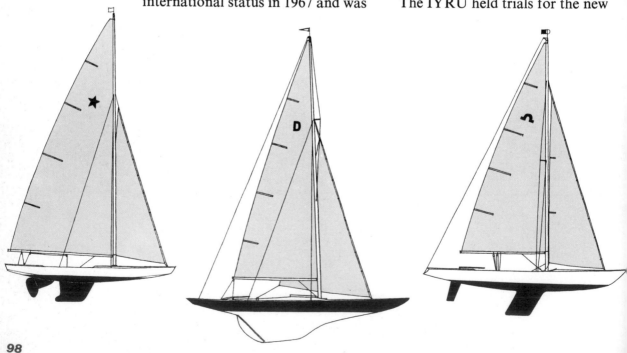

Two Dragons competing in a pre-Olympics trial.

The Soling class dinghy became an Olympic dinghy for the first time in 1972 at Kiel in Germany.

Star dinghies at the weather mark at Kiel, 1972. The Gold Medal was won by Forbes and Anderson of Australia.

Opposite: The Soling gold-medal-winning yacht at Kiel—the United States entry, sailed by Harry Melges.

boat in 1966 and although the Soling was the smallest of the fleet of new boats, her performance was considered to be sufficiently good to warrant her being included in further trials in 1967. During the winter of 1966–67 about 60 more Solings were built, and in 1967 after the next IYRU trials the Soling was adopted as an International Class yacht.

By 1968 there were over 300 Solings sailing all over the world and the International Olympic Committee, realizing the growing popularity of the boat, selected it for the 1972 Olympic Regatta. The average growth has been 500 boats a year built by licensed builders all over the world.

At their first Olympic appearance in 1972 at Kiel, the favourite to win was Denmark's Paul Elvström, the only man to win four Gold Medals in four consecutive Olympic Games. But the competition was so stiff that Elvström was pushed aside, and the Gold was won by Harry Melges Jr of the United

States. The Danes made a comeback in 1976 at Kingston, Canada, however, when Jensen won the Gold. The Silver at Kingston went to Kolius of the United States, and the Bronze to Below of East Germany.

The Soling seems set for a long Olympic career as the largest of the Olympic classes now that Dragons have been withdrawn. It is to be hoped that the boats will remain reasonably priced and will not tend, like so many other classes, to become cluttered with expensive extras and make winning more a question of having a well-padded wallet than being the most skilful man on the day.

The Tempest

The designated successor to the Star boats is the Tempest Class, another two-man keel boat of 6.7 metres (22 feet) over-all length. The Tempest was selected at an international trial held by the IYRU in Holland in 1965 to choose a new two-man Olympic keel boat. Sailed

by John Oakley and Cliff Norbury, the Tempest prototype won every race including the last one where it carried a 41 kg (80 lb) bag of sand as a handicap. Although the Tempest now replaces the Star, both boats were sailed in the 1972 Olympics and it was interesting to compare the differences between them. The Tempest was designed by Ian Proctor of Britain, and has all the latest techniques in so far as her mode of construction and method of sailing are concerned. The Star, although now built of GRP, misses out on the innovations. The most obvious is the omission of a trapeze for the crew. This enables the crewman to clip himself through a harness round his body on to a wire running from the top of the mast, in order that he can put his feet on the gunwhale and lean his whole body out from the side of the boat. The crew's weight applies a far greater momentum to keep the boat upright when right out overside like this, than can be expected from lying along the side of the deck as is the case with the Stars. The skipper in the Tempest can sit out on the gunwhale as can the skipper in the Star, but his boat is held nearer upright because of the better use of the crew's weight and except in very light airs the sails pull better if the boat is upright. Unlike the Star Class the Tempests have a spinnaker which is set, in addition to the jib and mainsail, when the boat is sailing off the wind. It enables a greater surface area to be set to catch the wind and increases the speed.

At Kiel, where like the Solings, the Tempests made their first appearance, the Gold Medal was won by Valentin Mankin of Russia, with the Silver going to Britain and the Bronze to the United States. At Kingston, John Albrechtsson of Sweden won the Gold, Mankin was forced down to second place for the Silver, and Dennis Conner of the United States took the Bronze. The Tempests have established themselves as a very fast and exciting Olympic class for both competitors and spectators alike.

Tempest
Length 6.7 m. 21.95 ft.
Beam 2.0 m. 6.46 ft.
Draught 1.1 m. 3.58 ft.
Displacement 470 kilos.
1035 lb.
Keel weight 229 kilos.
505 lb.
Sail area 22.9 sq. m.
247 sq. ft.

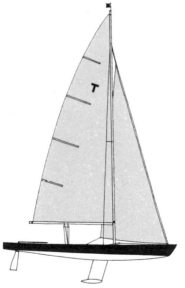

Flying Dutchman
Length 6.05m. 19.83 ft.
Beam 5.79 m. 19 ft.
Draught 1.2 m. 3.58 ft.
Weight 164.6 kilos. 374 lb.
Sail area 18 sq. m.
195 sq. ft.

The Flying Dutchman

The fastest and most exciting boat in the 1972 Olympics was the two-man dinghy, the Flying Dutchman, designed by Van Essen of Holland in 1957 and first sailed in the Olympics in 1960 in Italy. It has a retractable keel called a "centreboard" instead of the fixed keel used in all the classes mentioned so far. This centreboard, usually a steel plate, can be lowered or raised to provide both a grip in the water and a lowering of the centre of gravity for windward work, but it can be raised when the boat is running down wind and no grip is required and the least possible resistance is wanted.

The crewman has a trapeze as in the Tempest but needs to be a great deal more agile and fit as the Flying Dutchman is a very lively boat and has clocked speeds of up to 11 knots. At this speed there is no time for errors. The crewman cannot afford to be small either, as weight is imperative in order to keep the boat upright. To increase the crew's weight heavy jackets up to 66 kg (30 lb) are worn. Imagine wearing this jacket, leaping about for three or four hours in a heavy rubber wet suit, being constantly soaked with spray and all the time watching the boat's position relative to other

Competitors in the 1976 Olympic Games at Kingston in Canada.

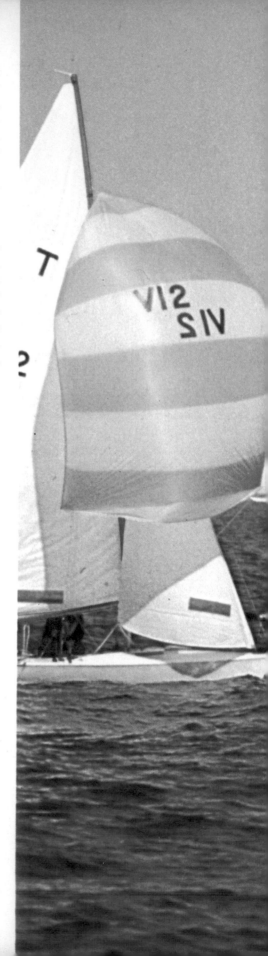

Tempests' spinnaker reaching in the 1972 Games. The eventual winners were Mankin and Dyrdyra of Russia, with Sweden taking the Silver Medal and Canada the Bronze.

boats, calculating the angles, and then having to anticipate your skipper's every thought. This will give you some idea of what is required from a top international Flying Dutchman crew. The skipper's task calls for no less strength, skill and concentration and the winner is the man who makes fewest mistakes.

It is interesting to compare the over-all weight of a Flying Dutchman Class dinghy with the keel boats mentioned so far—it is about one-third. This calls for a far greater effort on the part of the crew as he is, apart from the centreboard, the only means of keeping the boat upright and there is not the inherent stability that a fixed keel provides.

The man who dominated the Flying Dutchman Class for the eight years up to 1976 is Rodney Pattison of Great Britain. He won the Gold Medal at both the Mexican and Kiel Olympics. At Kingston, however, the West German Joerg Diesch managed a higher average over the seven races and took the Gold, with Pattison second for the Silver. Diesch overtook Pattison after the fifth race. Reinaldo Conrad of Brazil took the Bronze.

Finn, 470 and Tornado

The only single-handed dinghy in the Olympics was the result of the rule that the host nation to the Games may introduce one competition of its own choosing. In 1952 the Olympic Games were held in Helsinki, Finland, and the Finn's introduced a single-handed dinghy, called appropriately the Finn, as their choice. It has provided keen and exciting competition ever since.

The Finn Class differs from all

the other classes in the Olympics in that the boats are provided by the host nation. The helmsman receives his boat only a few days before the race and has no choice in the boat he will get. This gives the Finn Class a degree of competition unknown in other classes as all the helmsmen start out on equal terms.

The boat itself is a light-weight centreboard dinghy with an un-stayed swivelling mast. This means that unlike all other classes the mast has to be strong enough to support the sail without any help from rigging. Also, unlike other classes, the Finn dinghy has no headsail but relies entirely upon a mainsail as its sole means of propulsion.

Having only one man, the helmsman, the Finn calls for considerable ability as he has to double for the crew to sit out and keep the boat from capsizing, at the same time to steer, trim the sail and work out

Finn
Length 4.6 m. 14.75 ft.
Beam 1.6 m. 5.08 ft.
Draught 0.67 m. 21.5 ft.
Weight 159 kilos. 350 lb.
Sail area 10.5 m. 110 sq. ft.

Flying Dutchmen have been Olympic class since the 1960 Games in Rome.

his tactics. It was in a Finn that Paul Elvström won three of his Gold Medals in 1952, 1956 and 1960.

After the Olympic Games in 1972 the International Olympic Committee met and decided to withdraw the Dragon and Star Classes from future Olympic competition. There were considerable pressures from various international class associations, but finally the two new boats selected were the 470 and for the first time a multihull, the Tornado catamaran.

The 470 is a two-man centreboard dinghy which was brought in as an attempt to introduce a small cheap boat that was representative of the many classes of similar dinghies being sailed throughout the world. Once again, the Committee have picked a cheap boat to encourage greater international competition, particularly from the poorer nations where there are few, if any, people who could afford the more expensive Dragon. Unfortunately yet again, the wealthier yachting countries have forced up the price of the boat, but 28 entered at Kingston (a number only equalled by the Finns), and one can only hope that the numbers will continue to grow internationally and bring the price down. The Gold Medal was won by the West German Frank Huedner, the Silver by Spain's Antonio Gorostegui, and the Bronze by Ian Brown of Australia.

The Tornado catamaran was designed in Britain by Rodney March, Reg White and Terry Pearce for the IYRU trials held in 1967 to find an International B Class catamaran. The Tornado won the trials convincingly, although launched only two days before, and was selected. The class grew rapidly from 2 units in 1967 to 72 in 1968 and by 1971 nearly 900 boats were being sailed in areas as diverse as

Hawaii, Lebanon, South Africa, North America and Europe.

The World Champion of the class, and winner of the Gold Medal at Kingston was Reg White of Britain, one of the team who originally designed the boat. The Silver was won by David McFaull of the United States, and the Bronze by the West German Jorg Spengler. Now firmly established as an Olympic class, the Tornado provided probably the most spectacular sailing in the Games.

Finn dinghies at Kiel where Maury of France sailed to victory for the Gold Medal.

All the Olympic classes are internationally recognized and each holds its own World Championships at regular intervals in addition, but it is only at the Olympic Games that the six classes come together, bringing to one location every four years the world's top dinghy helmsmen to compete in what is still the world's premier sailing regatta.

Olympic Gold Medal Winners 1900–1936

Type of boat	1900 Paris (Le Havre) 6 nations	1908 London (Isle of Wight) 5 nations	1912 Stockholm (Nynashamn) 6 nations	1920 Antwerp (Ostend) 6 nations	1924 Paris (Le Havre) 19 nations	1928 Amsterdam (Zuidersee) 23 nations	1932 Los Angeles 11 nations	1936 Berlin (Kiel) 26 nations
0.5 Ton Class	France							
0.5–1.0 Ton Class	Great Britain							
1–2 Ton Class	Germany							
2–3 Ton Class	Great Britain							
3–10 Ton Class	USA							
10–20 Ton Class	France							
Open Class	Great Britain							
6 m (1907 type)		Great Britain	France	Belgium				
6 m (1919 type)				Norway	Norway	Norway	Sweden	Great Britain
6.5 m (1919)				Holland				
7 m (1907)		Great Britain		Great Britain				
8 m (1907)		Great Britain	Norway	Norway			USA	
8 m (1919)				Norway	Norway	France		Italy
10 m (1907)			Sweden	Norway				
10 m (1919)				Norway				
12 m (1907)		Great Britain	Norway	Norway				
12 m (1919)				Norway				
12 ft dinghy (1919)				Holland	Belgium	Sweden		
18 ft dinghy				Great Britain				
30-m² Class				Sweden				
40-m² Class				Sweden				
Snowbird							France	
Star							USA	Germany
Olympiajolle								Holland

The Olympic gold medal, Mexico 1968.

Opposite: Yves and Marc Pajot of France, Silver Medallists in their Flying Dutchman for France.

Olympic Gold Medal Winners 1948–1976

Type of Boat	1948 London (Torquay) 23 nations	1952 Helsinki (Harmaja) 29 nations	1956 Melbourne (Port Philip) 28 nations	1960 Rome (Neapel) 46 nations	1964 Tokyo (Enoshima) 40 nations	1968 Mexico City (Acapulco) 41 nations	1972 Munich (Kiel) 48 nations	1976 Montreal (Kingston) 28 nations
6 m (1919 type)	USA	USA						
Star	USA	Italy	USA	USSR	Bahamas	USA	Australia	
Firefly	Denmark							
Swallow	Great Britain							
Dragon	Norway	Norway	Sweden	Greece	Denmark	USA	Australia	
Finn		Denmark	Denmark	Denmark	West Germany	USSR	France	E Germany
5.5 m		USA	Sweden	USA	Australia	Sweden		
Sharpie			New Zealand					
Flying Dutchman				Norway	New Zealand	Great Britain	Great Britain	W Germany
Soling							USA	Denmark
Tempest							USSR	Sweden
470								W Germany
Tornado								Great Britain

CHAPTER 8

EPIC VOYAGES

The sea provides a unique challenge. Whereas the mountain-climber can rest at night on a piece of ground that will look basically the same the next day, the seafarer knows that at anytime the surface of the sea can change from being flat and meadow-like to being mountainous and dangerous within hours. Once a boat has been committed to a voyage, the crew know that their skills must be on call day and night, regardless of how tired or hungry they feel, until their destination is reached. It is this challenge, coupled with the feeling of satisfaction at a voyage's end, which makes ocean crossing one of the few real achievements left available in a world where most peaks have been climbed, rivers charted and jungles explored.

Ocean passages in small boats are nothing new. The Kon Tiki expedition was undertaken to show that in about AD 500 people set off across the Pacific from the west coast of South America in incredibly small and primitive rafts. We do not know why such a voyage was undertaken, but the reasons must have been strong for the sailors to take such risks.

More recently, several incredible small-boat voyages have been made. Captain Bligh of the mutiny on the *Bounty* fame, sailed 3,860 kilometres (2,400 miles) in a small open boat to safety after the mutineers forced him and a few loyal crew into one of the ship's boats.

Opposite: Robin Knox-Johnston heads for home, having almost completed the first solo non-stop circumnavigation of the world.

Conditions deteriorate very quickly at sea. Only hours before this photograph was taken the sea was quite calm. Within a short time the wind had risen to force 6 on the Beaufort Scale, the international measurement of wind strength.

But these voyages were, in one way or another, forced upon the sailors. It is only in the past 100 years that people have started making long ocean voyages in yachts because they wanted to rather than because they had to.

In most cases, the epic voyages have been undertaken by single-handers. For one person, sailing, maintaining and navigating a boat is incredibly hard work especially when the weather turns rough and sleep is next to impossible and there is no possibility of relief. In view of all the difficulties for the single-hander it is hard to appreciate that the longer voyages have only recently been undertaken by fully crewed boats. The pathfinding has, for some reason, been done by the single-handers. Although the world has been circumnavigated non-stop twice by single-handers, no fully crewed yacht has yet attempted it, and they have only recently even made the voyage half-way. One problem is, of course, the vast quantity of food required for a large crew on a long voyage; the other is obtaining a crew that are entirely compatible in confined conditions for long periods of time.

The voyages of Slocum and Voss

The earliest recorded ocean crossing by a single-hander was made by the American William Hudson in 1866 in a converted 8 metre (26 foot) long steel lifeboat called the *Red, White and Blue*. The boat, rigged as a full-rigged ship, which meant that all the sails were small and manageable, crossed the Atlantic from America to Britain in 36 days. This voyage attracted considerable interest in its day but it was not for ten years that anyone else tried, when Alfred Johnson made the same voyage in a 6 metre (20 foot) long gaff cutter.

The following year a third single-handed crossing was safely completed by Captain Thomas Crapo, this time in a 5.7 metre (19 foot) long boat.

Undoubtedly this aroused interest in single-handed ocean voyages and a number took place in the succeeding years, but it was not until 24 April, 1895 that the first single-handed circumnavigation of the world started.

The sailor, Captain Joshua Slocum, was an American master mariner who had already made a number of small-boat voyages with his family including one from Argentina and back to the United States with his wife and daughter. The boat he took round the world was the *Spray*, a 10.6 metre (35 foot) long gaff sloop which he entirely rebuilt with his own hands. Slocum bought the old frames of another boat, and, using them as a pattern, built the *Spray*.

His voyage began in Gloucester, Massachusetts and he ended the first leg in Gibraltar. From Gibraltar he sailed to Rio de Janeiro, being chased by Moroccan pirates on the way. After Rio he set sail for Chile via the Magellan Strait, defeating a raid by Indians by throwing tacks all over the deck so that when the raiders stepped aboard they got tacks in their feet and rapidly withdrew. After selling some tallow in Valparaiso which he had picked up from a wreck, Slocum sailed across the Pacific to Australia where he earned enough money by lecturing to carry on to South Africa. By now Slocum was well known, and was automatically taken to meet the redoubtable President Kruger in Johannesburg. Kruger believed the earth was flat and told Slocum that he was not sailing round the world at all, but round the edge of a flat plate!

The *Spray* finally dropped anchor in United States waters on 27 June, 1898, having narrowly escaped capture by Spanish warships with whom the United States was at war although Slocum knew nothing of it.

Slocum's circumnavigation was a thoroughly professional affair, carried out towards the end of the age of the days of sailing merchantmen, but achieved without the modern navigation aids that sailors today take so much for granted. The *Spray* disappeared at sea in 1909 when Slocum was on another solo voyage across the Caribbean.

Shortly after Slocum's circum-navigation Captain John C. Voss, a German sea-captain who had settled in Canada, set out from Vancouver in a converted dug-out canoe of 11.5 metres (38 feet) in length called *Tilikum* with a young companion called Norman Luxton. Voss must have been quite a character to live with as Luxton left him in Suva accusing him of just about everything from continuous drunkenness to attempted murder. Nothing daunted, Voss recruited a Frenchman, Louis Begent, and continued to Sydney, somehow losing Begent overside during the voyage. Voss sailed back

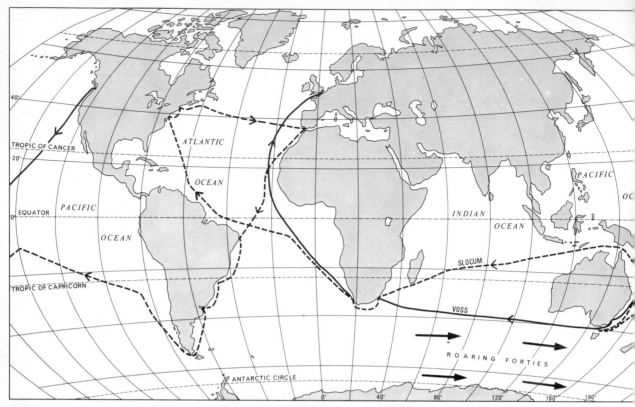

TROPIC OF CANCER

ATLANTIC

OCEAN

EQUATOR

PACIFIC

OCEAN

TROPIC OF CAPRICORN

PACIFIC

OCEAN

INDIAN

OCEAN

SLOCUM

VOSS

PACIFIC

OC

ANTARCTIC CIRCLE

ROARING FORTIES

to New Zealand where he recruited a new mate named MacMillan, and, with him sailed to South Africa. Here MacMillan left him, and recruiting yet another companion, Voss sailed on towards Europe finally dropping anchor off Margate on 2 September, 1904.

As Voss sailed in to Margate a voice called out, "Where are you from?"

"Victoria, British Columbia" Voss bellowed in reply.

"How long have you been on this voyage?"

"Three years, three months and twelve days", a reply that was greeted by a great cheer from the thousands who had come to watch.

Voss died in 1922 and six years later the *Tilikum* was rescued from the Thames mud and is now on display at the Maritime Museum at Victoria, British Columbia.

Great voyages of the twentieth century

In 1920 a 16 metre (52 foot) Brixham-type yawl named *Amaryllis* left Plymouth in England bound on what was to become the third circumnavigation by a small yacht. Skippered by George Muhlhauser, a retired British Naval Lieutenant, and with a crew of four others, she sailed across the Atlantic to the West Indies. Here Muhlhauser lost his crew and recruited a young Venezuelan sailor named Stephane, and a West Indian named Sam, and the three men sailed the *Amaryllis* to Tahiti. Muhlhauser's crew seemed to change frequently after this, one of the disadvantages of sailing a boat too large for one man, and he eventually arrived back in England with an Indian, Venezuelan, Moroccan and a Maltese named Galea.

Muhlhauser was a very different type of man to Voss. His behaviour was always impeccable, and he was retiring and shy, but above all he was a first-class seaman. He died shortly after his arrival home.

The relief at the end of World War I seems to have acted as a spur to a number of other men in addition to Muhlhauser. An Irishman, Conor O'Brien set off as *Amaryllis* was finishing her voyage in 1923, in a self-designed 12 metre (42 foot) built on the lines of an Arklow fishing smack. He called his boat *Saoirse*—Gaelic for freedom, which name was undoubtedly chosen to commemorate the recent establishment of the Republic of Ireland (Eire). O'Brien made the first circumnavigation that went south of the three Capes, Good Hope, Leeuwin and Horn. He also appears to have had trouble keeping a good crew together, and sailed the

Opposite above: The routes taken by Slocum and Voss in their early epic voyages.

Opposite below: Before he set out on his historic voyage, Robin Knox-Johnston had already sailed Suhaili from India to the UK.

Francis Chichester takes a sight aboard Gipsy Moth IV during his voyage. On his return to the UK, Chichester was knighted by Queen Elizabeth II of Great Britain in an historic outdoor ceremony at Greenwich.

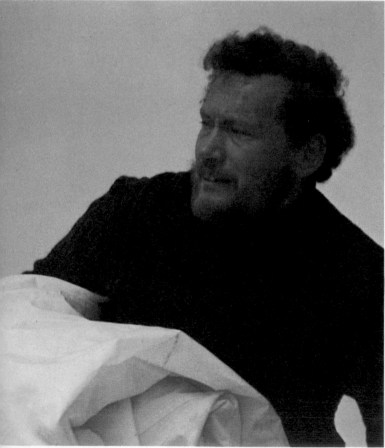

various legs with between two and four crew on board. In New Zealand he wrote "I am now resigned to looking for two more-or-less competent slaves." Nevertheless, he found crew for the remainder of his voyage round the Horn and home to Dublin. On arrival in Dublin he is quoted as saying "It is good to have sailed around the world in order to be home again!" O'Brien travelled 49,600 kilometres (31,000 miles) in 280 sailing days, averaging $5\frac{1}{4}$ knots, and making twelve stops.

Harry Pidgeon was an American who built his own dream ship, the *Islander*, a 10 metre (34 foot) yawl in eighteen months at the cost of $1,000 (£550). An attempt to reach Hawaii in a friend's boat convinced him of the advantages of sailing alone and in 1921 he left California for Hawaii in *Islander* alone. His voyage was, in comparison with some of the earlier circumnavigations fairly uneventful, but as he wrote himself:

"Ulysses is fabled to have had a very adventurous voyage while returning from the sack of Troy, but for sufficient reasons I avoided adventure as much as possible. Just the same, any landsman who builds his own vessel and sails alone around the world will certainly meet with some adventures so I offer no apology for my voyage. Those days were the freest and happiest of my life."

Pidgeon tried another circumnavigation in 1923 but the *Islander* was driven ashore in a typhoon. He planned another boat, but before he could finish it, died at the age of 81!

The 1930s produced many other circumnavigations, including a number of single-handed voyages, mostly sparked by the example of Slocum, and the publicity received by Muhlhauser, O'Brien and Pidgeon, but World War II brought this golden age of sailing to an end. During the war, an Argentinian,

Suhaili.

Opposite above: part of the self-steering gear on Chay Blyth's British Steel.

Opposite below: Robin Knox-Johnston working on board Suhaili. His voyage around the world took just under one year and he has said that the worst part of it was when he returned home and had to readjust to dealing with people after being on his own for so long.

Vito Dumas, set off round the world calling at Cape Town, Wellington in New Zealand, and Valparaiso in his 9.5 metre (32 foot) ketch *Legh II*, completing a circumnavigation with the fewest stops so far. It was not for over twenty years that the world was to be circumnavigated again single-handed.

Self steering

The main problem for the singlehander is how to keep his boat on course when he is doing something else like changing sail, eating, sleeping or navigating. In Slocum's time people were far more dependent upon the basic qualities of their boats to stay on course, and most boats were built with long keels anyway which gave considerable directional stability. Nowadays boats on the whole have shorter keels and so self-steering devices have been developed to give the helmsman some time free of steering. Self-steering devices work on the principle that once a boat has been set on course, the angle between the boat's course and the wind direction will be constant. If a balanced wind vane were to be set up on the boat it would always want to point straight at the direction from which the wind is blowing. If the boat swung off course, the vane would want to stay pointing into the wind, but this would change its position relative to the boat's fore and aft line. It is this movement, connected directly to a small rudder which is used to keep the boat on course. If the boat is on course, the vane will be in line with the wind and the small rudder lying fore and aft. When the boat swings off course, the vane will turn and this

Gipsy Moth IV moored in Sydney Harbour.

turns the rudder which will correct the boat's course. Obviously the vane will have to be adjusted depending on the wind's relative direction, but this is built into the equipment.

An epic race

In 1960 Lieutenant-Colonel "Blondie" Hasler, the man famous for the Commando raid in canoes up the Gironde during World War II, came up with the idea of a single-handed race across the Atlantic from England to the United States. Three men responded to the challenge, and eventually a British newspaper, the *Observer*, put up a small prize for the winner. The four starters were "Blondie" Hasler in *Jester*, Francis Chichester in *Gipsy Moth III*, David Lewis, a New Zealander, in *Cardinal Vertue* and Val Howells from Wales in *Eira*. Although the Atlantic had

been crossed on numerous occasions single-handed, each voyage had been an epic on its own; now an epic race was being planned. Francis Chichester was the first home after 40½ days, and Howell the last taking 63 days. All four arrived safely, and such was the reception, that it was decided to make an event of it every four years.

The second race in 1964 attracted 14 starters including all five competitors from the first race. The winner was Eric Tabarly of France in his ketch *Pen Duick II*, in the then incredible time of 27 days 3 hours 56 minutes. Francis Chichester in *Gipsy Moth III* came in second nearly three days later. All the starters, including three multihulls, finished the race safely.

By the start of the third Observer Single-handed Trans-Atlantic Race, or OSTAR as it had come to be called, in 1968, the event had become very popular, and 34 men and one

Chichester's round-the-world route.

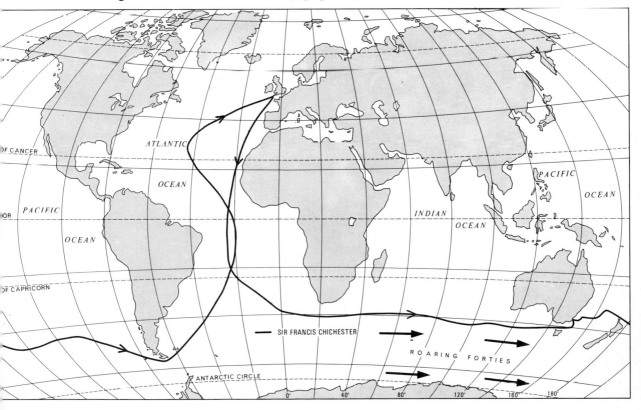

woman crossed the start line. Sponsored entries made their first appearance—this is one of the few events in sailing in which sponsorship is allowed—and as a result some much larger and more expensively fitted-out craft took part. Tabarly entered his new aluminium trimaran *Pen Duick IV*, favourite to win until forced to withdraw following a collision with a coaster shortly after the start. The winner, in a new record time of 25 days 20 hours 33 minutes was Englishman Geoffrey Williams in his 17 metre (56 foot) ketch *Sir Thomas Lipton*; second was South African Bruce Dalling in *Voortrekker*.

In 1972, the entry was up to 54 yachts—twenty-one British, thirteen French, five American, four Italian, three Polish, three West German, two Australian, and one each from Czechoslovakia, Holland and Belgium. But the numbers meant little as the French had entered by far the most formidable flotilla. The race to be first across the finish line was between Jean Terlain in the 38 metre (128 foot) monster three-masted schooner *Vendredi XIII* and Alain Colas in *Pen Duick IV*. Colas won in a new record time of 20 days 13 hours 15 minutes, while the enormous *Vendredi XIII* came home second, proving that it was possible for one man to handle such a large craft on his own, but leaving doubts as to whether the boat could be sailed efficiently enough to take advantage of the high hull speed made possible by the great length.

Both Colas and Terlain had obviously each been impressed by the other's efforts in 1972. In 1976, for the fifth OSTAR, Colas went for a giant monohull, a four-masted schooner named *Club Méditerranée*, which was 70·6 metres (236 feet) long and had a theoretical speed in excess of 20 knots; Terlain went for a

multihull and chartered *British Oxygen*, renaming her *Kriter III*. Interest in the race had grown to such an extent that nearly 200 boats entered; 125 started, divided into three classes with staggered starts as Plymouth Sound could not take all the competitors at one time! The largest class was for boats above 14 metres (46 feet) in length, the Pen Duick Class. Boats of between 8 and

14 metres (28 and 46 feet) in waterline length were in the Gipsy Moth Class; boats of under 10 metres (35 feet) in length were in the Jester class, which had by far the largest entry. A severe south-westerly storm hit the fleet when they were about a week out, and over 40 boats had to withdraw because of damage. A number of boats had to be abandoned including *Kriter III* which began to break up. The storm put paid to any hope of the 1972 record beating time, as all the boats had to heave to until it passed. *Club Mediterranée* looked like being the first home despite a 35-hour stop in St John's, Newfoundland to repair blown out sails and halyards. But at the last moment Eric Tabarly appeared over the horizon in *Pen Duick VI*, a 21 metre (70 foot) ocean

Sir Alec Rose prepares to set off on his voyage.

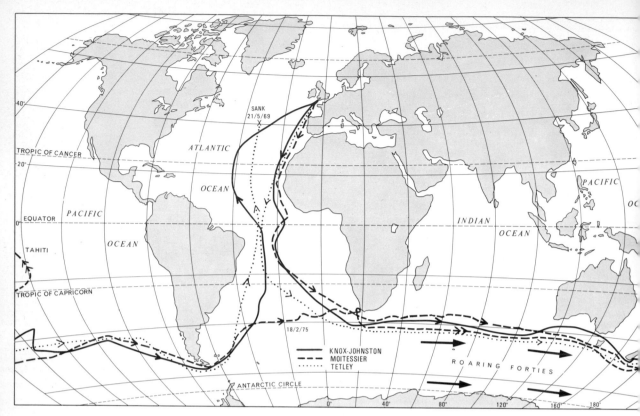

SANK
21/5/69
✕

TROPIC OF CANCER

ATLANTIC

OCEAN

PACIFIC

OCEAN

EQUATOR

TAHITI

PACIFIC

OCEAN

INDIAN

OCEAN

PACIFIC

OC

TROPIC OF CAPRICORN

18/2/75

KNOX-JOHNSTON
MOITESSIER
TETLEY

ROARING FORTIES

ANTARCTIC CIRCLE

0°   40°   80°   120°   160°   180°

Three of the round-the world race routes. Nigel Tetley's Victress *sank on 21 May 1969. Moitessier decided not to complete the race and sailed on to Tahiti. Robin Knox-Johnston finished the race and became the first person to complete a non-stop circumnavigation.*

Opposite above: The enormous Club Mediterranée.

Opposite below: Rehu Moana, *the multihull in which David Lewis and his family sailed round the world.*

racing monohull, and won by seven hours, even though he had been without his self-steering gear for 21 days. Tabarly thus became the only man to win the race twice. *Petrouchka* won the Gipsy Moth Class, and the Jester Class was won by Michael Birch of Canada in *The Third Turtle*, a 9 metre (31 foot) trimaran, which came in less than a day behind Colas.

If nothing else, the 1976 OSTAR proved that a small, efficiently sailed boat was a match for the giants, especially when really bad weather intervenes and puts extra strain on the skippers of the larger boats. The trend for the next OSTAR in 1980 may well be away from giants and back towards improved conventional sized boats. One hopes so. A single-hander has the right to risk his own life, but no right to risk other people's lives. In a small boat, a single-hander will nearly always come off worst in a collision, but in a

giant boat of, say, more than 30 metres (100 feet) in length, the single-hander, while asleep, could run down and sink a fishing boat or small coaster.

The Observer Single Handed Race re-established the cult of the single-hander, and lead to a number of solo voyages over various oceans, but in 1966 Chichester set out on what was to become the penultimate single-handed epic. Leaving Plymouth, England on 27 August, 1966 in his 16.5 metre (54 foot) *Gipsy Moth IV*, Chichester set off down the Atlantic past the Cape of Good Hope into the Roaring Forties and he did not stop until he reached Sydney, Australia. This voyage, by far the longest solo voyage made so far, was an incredible achievement especially when one considers that the sailor was 65 at the time. After only a month in Australia to repair his boat and rest, Chichester set off for England taking the hard route

round Cape Horn and arriving back in England on 28 May, 1967. It is difficult to appreciate fully the hardships and sheer dogged determination required to complete this voyage. Others sailed round the world stopping where their fancy took them to relax, rest and sightsee, sailing to see the world. Chichester sailed to circumnavigate the world.

Another Englishman, Alec Rose, had intended sailing at the same time as Chichester in his 11 metre (36 foot) yacht *Lively Lady* but had a collision on his way down the English Channel. Repairs delayed him a year, but in 1967 he set out again and this time reached Australia non-stop. His homeward passage was marred by damage sustained in the Tasman Sea which forced the sailor to seek repairs in Bluff, New Zealand. After these repairs he continued safely on round the world following the same route as Chichester and arriving home at Portsmouth on 4 July, 1968.

Racing round the world

These two circumnavigations left only one more voyage to be made, the circumnavigation of the world solo and non-stop. Already in 1967

a number of people were planning such a voyage, and in 1968 another British newspaper, the *Sunday Times*, saw the circulation value of the idea of another single-handed race, but this time round the world. Eventually nine people set off at various times during 1968 on what would be the last real epic. Of those who set out, only three even cleared the Atlantic on the way out. These were Bernard Moitessier of France in his steel ketch *Joshua*, 12 metres (39 feet) in length, a boat in which he had already sailed round the world; Commander Nigel Tetley in a slightly longer trimaran *Victress*, which had been his home for some years; and Robin Knox-Johnston, a British master mariner, in a 9.7 metre (32 foot) ketch *Suhaili* which he had sailed from India where the boat was built, the previous year.

Bernard Moitessier departed from Plymouth, England on 21 August, and made good time down the Atlantic. For some reason he slowed down across the Southern Ocean and passed New Zealand five weeks after Knox-Johnston. He had narrowed the gap by a further few days when he reached the Horn, and then, having passed the Falkland Islands, when, as far as he knew, there was no one in front of him, he suddenly decided not to return to Europe, but headed away into the Southern Ocean, past the Cape of Good Hope again and finally finished up in Tahiti. Moitessier is very much a man at home with the sea, and as such probably felt that the fuss that would surround his homecoming would constitute too much of an invasion of his privacy.

Nigel Tetley was the first man to circumnavigate the world in a trimaran, and nearly achieved the fastest circumnavigation. He left Plymouth on 16 September and by 11 January he was closing fast on Moitessier. He rounded the Horn on 18 March, almost two months after Knox-Johnston and headed up the Atlantic for home. All this time another competitor, Donald Crowhurst, had been cruising around the South Atlantic putting out false messages giving the impression that he was making a very fast circumnavigation. Thinking that Crowhurst could beat him, Tetley forced his battered boat into giving more speed and overstrained her. His hulls were leaking badly and he ran into a gale off the Azores which eventually caused further damage. Water started coming into the boat faster than he could pump it out. After quickly sending out a "Mayday" Tetley launched his liferaft, threw in his log-books and what equipment he could grab, and cast off from *Victress*. As he watched his home sink beneath the waves, Tetley set up his emergency radio transmitter and made contact. He was picked up a few hours later.

Robin Knox-Johnston sailed from Falmouth, England on 14 June, 1968. Two and a half months later while south of the Cape of Good Hope, his Atkins-designed Colin Archer-type boat *Suhaili* was knocked flat in the Roaring Forties. The damage sustained included the loss of all fresh water, the radio put out of order, and the cabin top shifted. Living off rainwater gathered in the sails, he continued on towards Australia and dropped off mail to the Melbourne pilot vessel. Off Otago in New Zealand he grounded briefly, but sailed off and continued on towards the Horn. At this time he seemed to be well in the lead of the other competitors. This was the last time he was seen for five months and no news was heard of him until 5 April, 1969 when he signalled a ship off the

Azores to report his position. He had rounded the Horn on 17 January completely unnoticed by the Chilean Navy who were looking for him. On 22 April he sailed the, by now, very tattered-looking *Suhaili* back into Falmouth. On being boarded by the Customs and asked where he was from he replied "Falmouth". The first single-handed non-stop circumnavigation of the world had been completed.

No greater distance remained to be sailed, but two years later another Briton, Chay Blyth, in a purpose-built steel ketch named *British Steel* sailed non-stop round the world from east to west. Much had been learned about boats and their equipment in recent years and Blyth's voyage proved that a well-designed boat, properly equipped, could circumnavigate the world non-stop without difficulty provided she was properly handled.

Even after the solo non-stop circumnavigations, when it appeared that there was nothing big left to do, restless spirits were looking for further challenges. David Lewis, the New Zealander of *Cardinal Vertue* and *Rehu Moana*

fame decided to try and circumnavigate the world below the parallel of 60° South Latitude. This does not seem very spectacular until you realize that it entails sailing continuously within the ice-belt round Antarctica. His boat the *Icebird* was especially fitted out for the voyage, but was badly smashed on the first leg and had to pull into an American Antarctic Station under jury rig for major repairs. The repairs were so drastic that he missed the summer that year and had to postpone the completion of his voyage until 1974. Again Lewis ran into trouble, and eventually his boat battered and himself near physical exhaustion, he headed for Cape Town and called off his attempt.

It is difficult for anyone else who has not seen the sea to appreciate the incredible difficulties that faced Lewis in his self-set task. There are places in the Antarctic which have an *average* wind force of Force 8, and what with these winds, blizzards and the continuous threat of ice, his target was one that few would set for themselves. Nevertheless, sooner or later someone will try.

APPENDIX I AMERICA'S CUP CHALLENGERS 1870–1974

Year	Course Length	No. of Races	Challenging Country	Challenger's Boat Name	Challenging Skipper	American Boat Name	American Skipper
1870	35.1	1	Britain	Cambria	J Linnock	Magic	A Comstock
1871	36.6	5	Britain	Livonia	J Woods	Columbia	N Comstock
						Sappho	J Greenwood
1876	36.3	2	Canada	Countess of Dufferin	J Ellsworth	Madeleine	J Williams
1881	32.3	2	Canada	Atalanta	A Cuthbert	Mischief	N Clock
1885	36.3	2	Britain	Genestra	J Carter	Puritan	A Crocker
1886	36.3	2	Britain	Galatea	D Bradford	Mayflower	M Stone
1887	36.3	2	Britain	Thistle	J Barr	Volunteer	H Haff
1893	30.0	3	Britain	Valkyrie II	W Cranfield	Vigilant	W Hansen
1895	30.0	3	Britain	Valkyrie III	W Cranfield	Defender	H Haff
1899	30.0	3	Britain	Shamrock	A Hogarth	Columbia	C Barr
1901	30.0	3	Britain	Shamrock II	E Sycamore	Columbia	C Barr
1903	30.0	3	Britain	Shamrock III	E Ringe	Reliance	C Barr
1926	30.0	5	Britain	Shamrock IV	W T Burton	Resolute	C Adams
1930	30.0	4	Britain	Shamrock V	T Heard	Enterprise	H Vanderbilt
1934	30.0	6	Britain	Endeavour	T Sopwith	Rainbow	H Vanderbilt
1937	30.0	4	Britain	Endeavour II	T Sopwith	Ranger	H Vanderbilt
1958	24.0	5	Britain	Sceptre	G Mann	Columbia	B Cunningham
1962	24.0	5	Australia	Gretel	J Sturrock	Weatherly	E Mosbacher Jnr
1964	24.3	4	Britain	Sovereign	P Scott	Constellation	R Bavier Jnr
1967	24.3	4	Australia	Dame Pattie	J Sturrock	Intrepid	E Mosbacher Jnr
1970	24.3	4	Australia	Gretel II	J Hardy	Intrepid	W Ficker
1974	24.3	4	Australia	Southern Cross	A Bond	Courageous	E Hood

ACKNOWLEDGMENTS

Ajax News and Features Service (Jonathan and Peter Eastland): pp. 4 (second top and bottom), 11, 13, 15 (top), 18, 22 (both), 23, 24 (both), 25 (bottom), 26, 30, 31, 34, 35, 36, 37, 38, 39, 40, 41, 42 (top and bottom), 43, 45 (top, centre and bottom), 46, 48 (top and bottom), 49, 50, 51 (right), 52 (bottom), 53, 55, 58–9, 60, 62, 63 (top and bottom), 64 (left), 64–5, 66 (bottom), 67, 68 (top and bottom), 69, 70, 71 (top), 72–3, 73, 74 (top and bottom), 75, 111, 113, 123 (top). Bob Fisher: pp. 96, 100, 101, 104–5, 106, 107, 108. Ambrose Greenway: pp. 25 (top), 54, 71 (bottom), 77, 99 (top and bottom). Keystone, Press: pp. 103, 109. Robin Knox-Johnston: pp. 56 (right), 116 (bottom). National Maritime Museum: pp. 4 (top), 8–9, 10 (both), 12 (top, centre and bottom), 15 (bottom), 78 (top and bottom), 80, 81, 82, 83 (top and bottom), 85, 87, 88–9. *Sunday Times*: pp. 16–17, 20, 21 (both), 27, 28 (all), 52 (top), 56 (left), 116 (top), 123 (bottom). G. L. Watson: pp. 4 (third top), 6. Camera Press: pp. 2, 7, 76, 86, 90, 92, 93 (top and bottom), 94, 95, 110, 114 (bottom), 115, 117, 118, 120–1.

The publishers gratefully acknowledge the assistance of Mr John Gardiner, Head of Design at Glasgow College of Technology, for the diagrams which appear on pp. 32, 33, 36, 51, 79, 98, 102, and 106; The Cartographic Department of the University of Strathclyde, Glasgow for the map on p. 66; and Mr Michael Shand of the Department of Cartography at Glasgow University for the maps on pp. 114, 119, and 122.

Cover: *Maverick*—a British contender for the Admiral's Cup Team. Photograph by Beken of Cowes.
Front Endpaper: Contenders in the One Ton Cup. Photograph by Jonathan Eastland. (paperback cover).
Back Endpaper: Sailing home in an autumn sunset. Photograph by Jonathan Eastland.

FURTHER READING

Reference sources

Bavier, Robert N., Jr. *The New Yacht Racing Rules, 1873–1976*. New York: W. W. Norton, 1974

Chamier, John. *Safety and Seamanship*. London: Adlard Coles, 1976

Hampton, T. A. *The Sailor's World: An Easy Guide to Ships, Harbors & Customs of the Sea*. N. Pomfret, Vt.: David & Charles, 1972

Heaton, Peter. *Sailing*. London: Penguin, 1976

Kinsey, T. L. *Family Cruising*. London: Stanley Paul, 1975

Rather, A. A. *Signalman's Training Kit*. Cambridge, Md.: Cornell Maritime Press, 1944

U.S. Coast Guard Transport Dept. *Simple Guide to Safer Sailing & Boating*. New York: Arco, 1974

Webb, Barbara. *Yachtsman's Eight Language Dictionary*. Atlantic Highlands, N.J.: Humanities Press, 1965

Sailing, Small Boat Handling, Racing

Adkins, Jan. *The Craft of Sailing*. New York: Walker & Co., 1973

Blandford, Percy W. *The Art of Sailing*. New York: St Martin's Press, 1971

Chamier, John. *Small Boat and Dinghy Sailing*. London: Pelham Books, 1963

Bruce, Errol. *Deep Sea Sailing*. London: Stanley Paul, 1973; Tuckahoe, N.Y.: John De Graff, 1967

Clark, Lincoln and Clark, Alice. *ABC's of Small Boat Handling*. Garden City, N.Y.: Doubleday, 1963

Colgate, Stephen, *Colgate's Basic Sailing Theory*. New York: Van Nostrand Reinhold, 1973

Drummond, A. H., Jr. *The Complete Beginner's Guide to Sailing*. New ed. Garden City, N.Y.: McKay, 1975

Duxbury, Ken. *Dinghy Sailing*. London: Pelham Books, 1972

Editors of *Rudder. Good Sailing: An Illustrated Course on Sailing*. New York: McKay, 1975

Henderson, Richard. *Hand, Reef and Steer: A Practical Handbook for Sailing*. Chicago: Henry Regnery, 1965

Hiscock, Eric C. *Voyaging Under Sail*. 2nd ed. New York: Oxford University Press, 1970

Knapp, Arthur, Jr. *Race Your Boat Right*. 3rd ed. New York: Grosset & Dunlap, 1973

Law, Donald. *The Beginner's Guide to Sailing*. London John Gifford, 1974

Moore, J. B. *Small Boat Racing*. London: Stanley Paul, 1967

Schult, Joachim. *Tactics and Strategy in Yacht Racing*. Tr. by Barbara Webb. New York: Dodd Mead, 1971

Watts, Alan. *Wind & Sailing Boats: The Structure and Behaviour of the Wind as it affects Sailing Craft*. New York: Quadrangle/New York Times Co., 1967

Aids to Navigation

Farrell, Charles. *Fell's Guide to Small Boat Navigation*. Rev. ed. New York: Magnet Books, 1974

Gibbs, Tony. *Navigation: Finding Your Way on Sea and Land*. (Impact Books) New York: Franklin Watts, 1975

Harvey, D. O. *Yachting & Boating Book of Navigation*. London: Sphere Books, 1974

Townsend, Sallie and Ericson, Virginia. *The Amateur Navigator's Handbook*. New York: T. Y. Crowell, 1974

Voyages and Epic Voyages

Blyth, Chay. *Theirs is the Glory*. London: Hodder & Stoughton, 1974

Chichester, Francis. *The Romantic Challenge*. New York: Coward, McCann & Geoghegan, 1972
Alone Across the Atlantic. London: Allen & Unwin, 1968
"Gipsy Moth" Circles the World. London: Hodder & Stoughton, 1967/Pan, 1969
Lonely Sea and the Sky. London: Hodder & Stoughton, 1964/Pan, 1967

Heaton, Peter. *The Singlehanders*. London: Michael Joseph, 1976

*Heyerdahl, Thor. *Kon-Tiki*. Chicago: Rand McNally, 1950
Ra Expeditions. Tr. by P. Crampton. London: Allen & Unwin, 1971/Penguin, 1973

Knox-Johnston, Robin. *World of My Own*. New York: William Morrow, 1970; London: Corgi, 1971
Robin Round the World. London: Cassell, 1970

Leslie, Anita. *Francis Chichester*. New York: Walker & Co., 1975

*Nordhoff, Charles & Hall, James N. *The Bounty Trilogy*. Boston: Little, Brown, 1946

Page, Frank. *Solo to America*. London: Adlard Coles, 1972

*Phillips-Birt, D. *The Love of Sailing*. London: Octopus, 1976

Rogers, Woods. *Cruising Voyage Round the World*. New York: Dover, 1970

Slocum, Joshua. *Sailing Alone Around the World*. New York: Macmillan, 1970

* Less technical and simpler reading

INDEX
Italic page numbers indicate an illustration

Admiral's Cup, *61, 62*, 66–9, *67, 70, 71*;
  course *67*
Adventure, 80, 81, *87*
Aerofoils, 41, 44, *44*, 45
Amaryllis, 115
America, 10, 11, *11, 77*, 77–9
American Universal Rule, 14
America's Cup, 11, 15, 77–95, *79*;
  challengers, *125*
Anemometer, 75
Anker, Johan, 98
Apache Class, 42
Ashbury, James, 79–81
Astro-navigation, 57
Atalanta, 80, 81, *87*
Atlantic, 16
Aurora, 77
Avenger, 19

B
Backstay, 22
Ballast, 35, 36
Bearings, 55
Beaufort Scale, 111
Bendy mast, 97
Bermuda Race, 16, 61, 62
Bermudan rig, 14, *21*, 22, *59*, 97
Bloodhound, 16, 62
Blyth, Chay, *117*, 122, 123
Boom 23
Bounty, 111
Boyd, David, 92
Britannia, 7, 14, *15*
Britannia Cup, 66
British Oxygen, 40, 43, 120
British Steel, 117
Buoys, 54
Burton Cutter, 71, 72

C
Cambria, 78, 79
Camille of Seaforth, 67
Canoe stern, 47–9
Cape-Rio Race, 70
Caprice of Huon, 67
Capsizing, *28*, 29
Cardinal Vertue, 119, 125
Carina, 61
Catamaran, 35, *36*, 36–40, *43*; Apache Class,
  42; C Class, 40, 41; Hobie Cat, 37;
  Tornado, 37, *37*, 40, 104–7; Unicorn, *38*
Centreboard, 24–5, *24*, 103
Channel Race, 66
Charles II, 7, *7*, 8
Charts, 54, *56*
Chichester, Sir Francis, 115, 119, *119*, 120
Classes 14, 72, *75*; dinghy, 19, *30*, 31, 32, 33;
  Dragon, 97, 98, *98, 99*; Finn, 97, *103*,
  104–7, *106, 107*; Flying Dutchman, 97, *97*,
  102–4, *102, 106*; J, 14, 90, 91; Soling, 97–
  100, *98, 99, 100*; Star, 97, *98, 100*; Tempest,
  97, 100–2, *102, 104*; Tornado, 104–7;
  4 metre, 17; 12 metre, *15*, 90–5
Clifton Flasher, 45
Clinker built, 20
Club Méditerranée, 120–1
Coffee grinders, 74, *75*
Colas, Alain, 40, 41, 120
Columbia, 80, 86, 91
Compulsory buoyancy, 97
Cona, 13
Constellation, 92
Countess of Dufferin, 80
Courageous, 94, 95
Cowes Week, 66
Cringle, 23
Crossbow, 44, 45

Cruising, 47–59; boat-types, 47–9;
  check-list, 49–51; provisions, 57–9; safety,
  51–3, *53*
Crystal Trophy, 41
Cunningham hole, 23
Cutters, 8, 11, 14

D
Dalling, Bruce, 120
Dame Pattie, 93, 94
Dauntless, 78, 79
Day, T. F., 61, 62
Deck fittings, 22
Dinghy, 16, 17, 19–33; choosing a, 30, 31;
  classes, 19, *30*, 31, 32, 33; clinker built, 20,
  21, General Purpose, *19, 24, 30*; Inter-
  national Snipe, 20; International, 14, 19,
  30; materials, 20, 31; sails, 20 4; V section,
  17; 4 metre, 19
Distress flares, 52, 53
Dorade, 62
Downie, Rod Macalpine, 45
Dragon Class, 97, 98, *98, 99*
Dumas, Vito, 118

E
Earl of Dunraven, 83, *85*
Easterner, 91
Echo sounders, 55, 75
Edward VII, 14
Eira, 119
Elvström, Paul, 100, 107
Endeavour, 14, 88–91
Enterprise, 88

F
Falcon, 10
Fastnet Race, *16*, 17, 62, 63, 66
Felucca, *22*
Fife, William, 17, 85
Financial Times, 35, 41
Finn Class, 97, *103*, 104–7, *106, 107*
Finrose, 37, *51, 59*
Fishing, 58
Flags, signal 56, 57
Flying Dutchman, *22, 24*, 97, *97*, 102–4, *102,
  106*
Foot, 22
Forestay, 22
Fox, Uffa, 17, 19, 63
France, 94
Freya, 67

G
Gaff rig, 21, 22, 97
Galatea, 81, *81*, 82
General Purpose dinghy, *19, 24, 30*
Genesta, 81, 82, *88*
George IV, 9
Gipsy Moth III, 119; *IV, 115, 118*, 119, 120
Gooseneck, 23
Gretel, 77, 91, 92, *93; II* 94
Gunter rig, 21, 22

H
Half Ton Cup, *73*
Hallowe'en, 17
Halyard, 22; main, 23
Handicap rules, 11–14, 61
Hanks, 22
Hard chine, 20
Hasler, "Blondie", 119
Herreshof, Nathaniel, 36, 84–7
Hobie Cat, 37
Hood, Ted, 95
Horizontal sextant angles, 57
Horse, 23

Howells, Val, 119
Hudson, William, 112
Hydrofoils, 43, 44, *44*

I
Icebird, 125
Ilex, 17
International Catamaran Challenge Cup, 40,
  41
International flag code, 56
International Offshore Committee, 17
International Offshore Rule, 61, 86
International Snipe, 20
International Yacht Racing Union, 14
International 14 dinghy, 19, 30
Intrepid, 94
Iselin, C. Oliver, 84, 86
Islander, 116

J
J Class, 14, 90, 91
Jester, 119
Jib, 22, *22*
Jolie Brise, 17, 62
Joshua, 124

K
Kaiser Wilhelm, 7, *7*, 16
Kemp, Dixon, 14
Knox-Johnston, Robin, 42, 43, *111, 115, 117*,
  121–3
Kon Tiki, 111
Kriter III, 120–1
Kurrewa II, 95; V 92

L
Lady Helmsman, 44
Lateen, 20, 21, *22*
Leach, 22
Lead lines, 55
Legh II, 118
Level Rating Racing, 73
Lewis, David, 58, 59, 119, *122*, 125
Lifejackets, 29, 51
Linge, Jan Herman, 98
Lipton, Sir Thomas, 85–8
"Little Ships" race, *30*
Lively Lady, 112
Livonia, 78, 79, 80, *82*
Lugsail, 21; dipping, 21; standing, 21, *23*
Lulworth, 9, *12*

M
Madeleine, 80
Mandamm, 10
Mainsail, dinghy, 23
Manureva, 40
March, Rodney, 107
Marconi rig, 14
Martin, George, 17, 62
Mary, 7, *12*
Mayflower, 82
Mayfly, 44
McMullen, Mike, 42, 43
Melges, Buddy, *100*
Middle Sea Race, 70
Mischief, 81, *87*
Miss Nylex, 44
Moitessier, Bernard, 124
Morgan, J. P., 11, 86
Morning Cloud, 71
Morse code, 56
Mosbacher, Bus, 91, 92
Muhlhauser, George, 115
Multihull, 35–45; development, 43; races,
  40–3
Murray, Hugh, *44*

N

National Survey Charts, 54
Navigation, 53–5, 57
New York Yacht Club Cup, 66
Newish, Dick, 42
Nicholson, Charles, 17, 62, 87–9
Notices to Mariners, 54
Nova 2, 44

O

O'Brien, Conor, 115, 116
Observer Single Handed Race (OSTAR), 119–22
Ocean-going rig, 73–6
Ocean racing, 61–75
Ocean Racing Club, 17, 62
Ocean Spirit, 42, *42*
Offshore racing, *see* Ocean racing
Olympic classes, 97–109
Olympic gold medal winners, 109
Outrigger, 36

P

Packer, Sir Frank, 91, 92, 94
Pattison, Rodney, 104
Payne, Alan, 91
Pearce, Terry, 107
Pen Duick II, 119; *IV*, 120; *V*, 41; *VI* 67, 121
Perseverance, 75
Pidgeon, Harry, 116
Pinta, 71
Planesail, 44
Planing, 17, 19, 20, *36*
Prince Albert, 10
Proas, 36, 45
Proctor, Ian, 102
Provisions for cruising, 57–9
Puritan, 81, 82, *88*

R

Racing, dinghy, 16, 17; history of, 8–17, *9*; multihull, 40–3; offshore, 16, 17, 61–75
Radio Direction Finder, 55, 75
Radio-telephone, 56, 57, *56*
Ragamuffin, 69
Rainbow, 89, 90
Ranger, 91
Rat of Wight, 7
Red Rooster, 69
Red, White and Blue, 112
Reefing, 24; points, 24; roller, 24; slab, 24
Rehu Moana, 58, *122*, 125
Reliance, 86
Resolute, 87

Rigs, Bermudan, 14, 21, 22, *59*, 97; dinghy, 20, 21; gaff, 21, 22, 97; gunter, 21, 22; lateen, 20, 21, *22*; lugsail, 21, *23*; Marconi, 14; ocean-going, 73–6; sloop, *20*
Rose, Sir Alec, *112, 121*, 123
Round Britain Race, 42, *42*, 43
Royal Cork Yacht Club, 8
Royal Ocean Racing Club, 17, 62
Royal Yacht Squadron, 9
Rudders, dinghy, 25, *25*

S

Safety, 27–30, *28*, 51–3, *53*
Sailing points, *51*
Sails, *20*, 74; design, 44; dinghy, 20–4, *20*
Salty Goose, 71
Saoirse, 115
Sappho, 80, *82*
Saudade, 70
Sayula, 72, 75
Sceptre, *90*, 91, *95*
Schooner, 10, 11, 16
Scott, Peter, 92
Self-steering, 118, 119
Sextant, *54*; 57; angles, 57
Shamrock, *14*, 85–8
Sheets, 20
Shrouds, 22
Signalling, 56, 57
Sir Thomas Lipton, 120
Slocum, Captain Joshua, 112–14, *114*
Snipe, 20
Soling Class, 97–100, *98, 99, 100*
Sopwith, Sir Thomas, 88–90
South Coast One Design, *13*, 14
Southern Cross, 94, *94*, 95
Southern Cross Series, 62
Southern Lion, 35
Sovereign, 92
Spinnakers, 26, *26*, 27, 64, *64, 65*
Spray, 112, 113
Star Class, 97, *98, 100*
Stays, 22
Stephens, Olin, 17, 62, 91
Stormy Weather, 62
Suhaili, *117*, 124
Sunday Times race, *122*, 122–4
Sutton, Sir Richard, 81
Sweisguth, Francis, 19, 97
Sydney-Hobart Race, 62

T

Tabarly, Eric, *67*, 119–20
Tempest 97, 100–2, *102, 104*
Teelain, Jean, 120

Tetley, Nigel, 124
Third Turtle, The, 122
Thistle, 82
Three Cheers, *42*
Tilikum, 113
Tillers, 25
Toe straps, 97
Tonnage, 13, 14
Toria, 42
Tornado, 37, *37*, 104–7
Transpac Race, 62
Trapeze, 25, 38, *38*
Trimaran, *35*, 36, *36*, 42
Trumpeter, 42
Twelve metre Class, *15*, 90–5

U

Unicorn catamaran, *38*
Universal J Class Rule, 87, 88
Universal Rule, 86

V

Valkyrie 15; II, 82, 83, 84; *III*, 84, 85, *85*
Valsheda, 14
Van Essen, 103
Vendredi XIII, 120
Vertical sextant angles, 57
Victress, 121
Vigilant, *15*, *82*, 83, 84
Vim, *77*, 91
Volunteer, *82*
Voortrekker, 120
Voss, Captain John C., 113–15, *114*
V-section dinghy, 17

W

War Baby, *15*
Waterwitch, 9, *12*
Watson, George L., 86
Weatherly, 91, 92
Weld, Phil, 42
Westerly Medway, *50*
Westerly Tiger, *48*
Whitbread Round the World Race, *67*
White Ensign, 10
White, Reg, 107
Williams, Geoffrey, 120
Wyatt, Sir Myles, 66

Y

Yachts, history of, 7–17
Yankee Girl, 62
Yeoman XX, 69